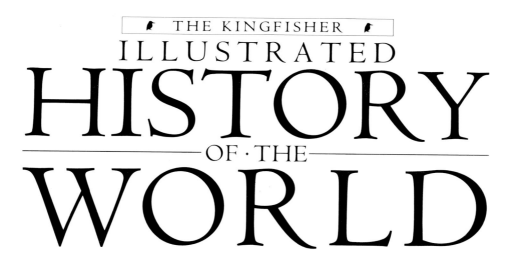

THE KINGFISHER
ILLUSTRATED
HISTORY
OF · THE
WORLD

General Editor: Charlotte Evans

The Renaissance
1461–1600

5

Kingfisher Books

Kingfisher Books, Grisewood & Dempsey Ltd,
Elsley House, 24-30 Great Titchfield Street, London W1P 7AD

First published in 1992 by Kingfisher Books

British Library Cataloguing-in-Publication Data
A catalogue record for this book is available from the British Library

ISBN 0 86272 792 8

Typeset by Tradespools Ltd, Frome, Somerset
Printed in Italy

Contents

The Renaissance

The period from 1461 to 1600 marks the start of modern history. Europeans started to emerge from the narrow confines of the Middle Ages to travel beyond their own continent. The movement now called the Renaissance began when Greek scholars, fleeing from the fall of Constantinople to the Ottoman Turks, brought with them the knowledge of ancient Greece and Rome. Education, art, science and architecture were all affected as people began to question what they were told.

Unknown to most Europeans at the start of this period, other civilizations were flourishing elsewhere in the world. In India the Mogul empire was founded. It expanded under the rule of wise emperors who, although Muslim themselves, treated their Muslim, Hindu and Sikh subjects equally.

In the Far East, China was fairly peaceful and prosperous under the rule of the Ming, but Japan was being torn apart by civil wars as its feudal lords struggled with each other for control.

From 1460 European explorers set out to find new routes to the Far East. The Portuguese sailed south along the coast of Africa and on to reach the Moluccas, China and Japan. Trading posts were established but settlers were rarely allowed further than the coast. In contrast, the Spanish set out to conquer the lands they explored. When Columbus arrived in the West Indies in 1492 he claimed them for Spain, although the Arawak and Carib Indians already lived there. By 1535 the Spaniards had turned the people of South and Central America into slaves; the original inhabitants were nearly wiped out by disease and ill-use.

▼ *The Renaissance was a time of great prosperity in Italy, but some Christians condemned the luxury and vanity of the rich. One such was Savonarola, who ruled Florence from 1494 to 1498. He had great bonfires built on which people burnt their precious possessions.*

The Americas

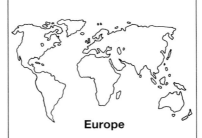

Europe

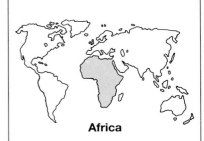

Africa

1466 The Incas under Topa overrun the Chimu empire.

1492 Christopher Columbus reaches the Caribbean islands.
1494 The Treaty of Tordesillas divides the known world between Spain and Portugal.
1498 Huayna Capac extends the Inca empire into Colombia.
1503 Montezuma becomes ruler of the Aztecs.
1521 Hernán Cortés conquers the Aztec empire.
1525 Civil war in Inca empire.
1533 Francisco Pizarro conquers the Inca empire.
1535 Large silver mines are discovered in Peru and Mexico. The local people are forced to work in them, but the silver is sent to Spain.
1535–1536 Jacques Cartier sails to Canada and explores the St Lawrence River.

c. 1570 The Portuguese set up the first sugar plantations in Brazil.
1585 Sir Walter Raleigh tries to set up an English colony in Virginia but fails.

1462 Ivan III becomes ruler of Muscovy and much of Russia is freed from Tartar control.
1485 The end of the Wars of the Roses in England.

1517 Martin Luther, a German priest, starts the Reformation.
1519 Charles I of Spain becomes Charles V of the Holy Roman Empire.
1529 The Ottoman Turks beseige Vienna.
1534 Henry VIII becomes head of the Church in England.
1543 Nicolas Copernicus states that the Earth moves round the Sun.
1545 The first meeting of the Council of Trent starts the Counter-Reformation.
1562–1598 Wars of Religion in France.
1568 A revolt against Spain starts in the Netherlands.
1571 The battle of Lepanto ends Ottoman ambitions in the Mediterranean.
1588 Defeat of the Spanish Armada in the English Channel.
1600 Foundation of the English East India Company.

1464 The kingdom of Songhay becomes independent of the Mali empire in West Africa.
1482 The Portuguese start to settle the Gold Coast (Ghana).
1488 Bartolomeu Dias sails round the Cape of Good Hope.

1502 The first African slaves are taken to work in the Americas.
1505 The Portuguese set up trading posts along the east coast of Africa.

1571 In the Sudan the Kanem Bornu empire flourishes.
1574 The Portuguese colonize Angola in southern Africa.
1578 The Moroccans destroy Portuguese power in north-western Africa.
1591 The Moroccans overrun the Songhay empire.
1600 In West Africa the Oyo empire starts to flourish.

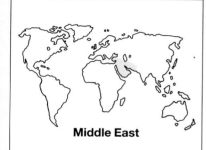

Middle East

Asia and the Far East

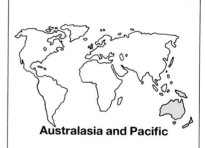

Australasia and Pacific

1463–1479 War between Ottoman empire and Venetians.

1471 The Vietnamese conquer their neighbours the Champa.

1498 Vasco da Gama reaches India.
1512 Portuguese traders reach the Moluccas.
1519 Guru Nanak founds the Sikh religion in India.
1526 Babur conquers Delhi and founds the Mogul empire.

1501 The Safavid dynasty is founded in Persia (Iran).
1520 Suleiman I becomes sultan of the Ottoman empire.
1526 Ottomans defeat Hungary at the battle of Mohacs.

1534 Suleiman conquers Baghdad in the Safavid empire.

1520 Ferdinand Magellan sails around Cape Horn and into an ocean which he names the Pacific. He then sails north-east until he reaches the Philippines where he is killed.

1542 Portuguese explorers arrive in Japan.
1549 Jesuit missionaries arrive in Japan and start converting the people to Christianity.
1550 The Mongols under Altan Khan invade northern China.

1566 The golden age of the Ottoman empire ends.

A Turkish velvet, saddle-cover.

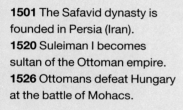

1571 Spain conquers the Philippines.
1581 Russian settlement of Siberia starts.
1592–1593 The Japanese invade Korea, but are defeated by the Chinese.

An Aboriginal bark drawing of a lightning spirit

The World

In 1461 European seafarers, traders and colonists were on the brink of setting out to explore and exploit the rest of the world. For the first time continents were brought into direct contact with each other.

In **Central** and **South America** the Aztec and Inca empires were at their height, but with the arrival of Europeans the Aztec capital Tenochtitlán was destroyed and the Incas were forced to retreat to the highlands of Peru. The invaders turned their attention north, but it was not to be for several decades that **North America** would feel the real effects of their arrival.

African civilizations too came under European influence, but it was confined to the coast. The heart of **Africa** remained, for now, undisturbed.

China was still ruled by the Ming. Although the arts flourished, society had begun to stagnate under their rule.

In **Europe** itself the new ideas led some people to question their religion. By 1600 half the population of Europe had left the Catholic Church and joined a new one: the Protestants.

◀ *Native North Americans respected nature. They believed a supernatural force linked humans to every other thing. For this reason one of the tribe's most important members was the medicine man.*

NORTH AMERICA

Aztec empire

CENTRAL AMERICA

PACIFIC OCEAN

Inca empire

SOUTH AMERICA

▼ *The Native people of South and Central America were forced to work in silver mines for the profit of their Spanish conquerors. Many died under the harsh conditions.*

▲ *In the early hours of 12 October 1492 Christopher Columbus's crew first sighted the New World, the continent of America.*

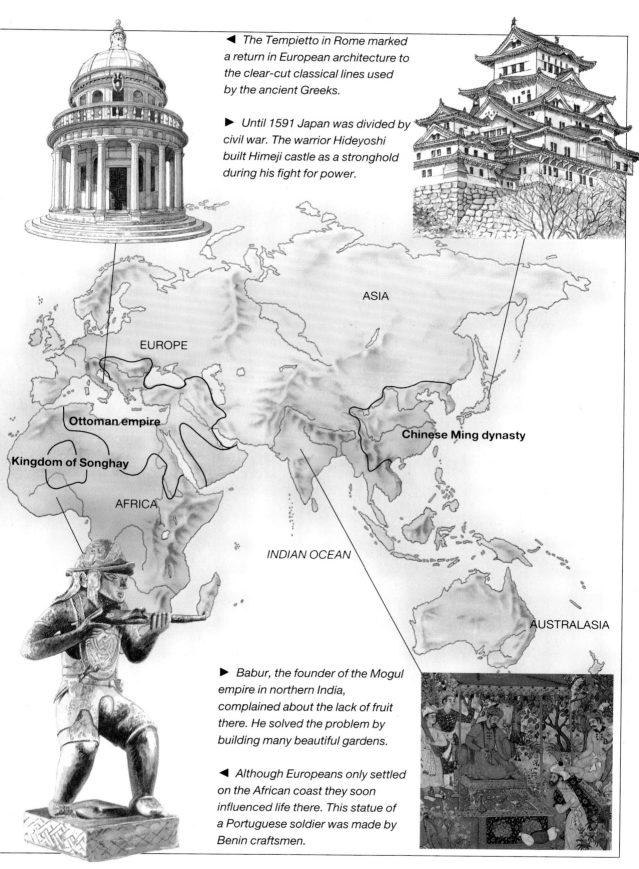

◀ The Tempietto in Rome marked a return in European architecture to the clear-cut classical lines used by the ancient Greeks.

▶ Until 1591 Japan was divided by civil war. The warrior Hideyoshi built Himeji castle as a stronghold during his fight for power.

ASIA

EUROPE

Ottoman empire

Kingdom of Songhay

Chinese Ming dynasty

AFRICA

INDIAN OCEAN

AUSTRALASIA

▶ Babur, the founder of the Mogul empire in northern India, complained about the lack of fruit there. He solved the problem by building many beautiful gardens.

◀ Although Europeans only settled on the African coast they soon influenced life there. This statue of a Portuguese soldier was made by Benin craftsmen.

1461 England: The Wars of the Roses between the Houses of Lancaster and York continue. With the help of the Earl of Warwick, also known as the Kingmaker, Richard of York's son, Edward, defeats the Lancastrians at the battle of Towton in March and becomes King Edward IV of England (to 1470). France: Louis XI is king (to 1483). Ottoman empire: The Ottoman Turks conquer Trebizond (now called Trabzon), Turkey, the capital of the Comnenian empire since 1204.

c. 1461 Central America: The Aztec empire is at its height.

1462 Russia: Ivan III, also known as Ivan the Great, becomes duke of Muscovy (to 1505). His capital is Moscow. Spain: the kingdom of Castile captures Gibraltar from the Arabs.

The hideously grinning skull face of the Aztec god of death is shown in this terracotta statue. The Aztecs also used human skulls to make masks. They encrusted them with turquoise and sea shells and lined the inside with red leather.

1463 War starts between the Ottoman Turks and the Venetians (to 1479). South America: Pachacuti, the Sapa Inca, wages war, successfully, against the Lupaca and Colla tribes. Quechua, the Inca language, is established in his empire. Pachacuti gives control of the Inca army to his son, Topa.

1464 Papal States: Paul II becomes pope (to 1471). England: Edward IV marries Elizabeth Woodville. West Africa: Sonni Ali becomes ruler of Songhay and makes it independent of the empire of Mali. Sonni Ali also begins to enlarge Songhay's boundaries.

The Aztec Empire

By the end of the 15th century, the Aztecs controlled a large empire in Central America. Its capital Tenochtitlán is estimated to have had a population of 150,000 people. In order to feed them all, food was grown on artificial islands, or chinampas, constructed in the lake in the middle of which the city stood (*see* page 268).

Peoples who had been conquered by the Aztecs brought food as tribute. They provided maize (corn), beans and cocoa, cotton cloth, as well as gold, silver and jade for the Aztec craftsmen.

Traders brought turquoise from the Pueblo Indians to the north of the Aztec empire, while from the south came brightly coloured feathers. The feathers were used to make elaborately decorated capes, fans, shields and headdresses.

Aztec society was organized along military lines. All boys had to serve in the army from the age of 17 to 22. Some stayed on longer than this, because even a peasant could rise to be an army

▲ *From their capital of Tenochtitlán, the Aztecs dominated most of the lands between the Gulf of Mexico and the Pacific Ocean.*

▶ Priests were a very special class of people in Aztec society. They were responsible for making the human sacrifices to keep the gods happy. Since they did not know how to use metal for making tools, the priests used stone-bladed knives on their victims.

▲ This headdress from the 16th century is made mainly of quetzal feathers. Parrot feathers in brown, crimson, white and blue were also used.

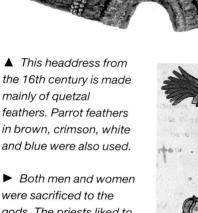

▶ Both men and women were sacrificed to the gods. The priests liked to kill a victim by cutting out the living heart so that it jumped out of the body. Thousands of people might be killed in a day.

commander if he tried hard enough.

One of the main tasks of the Aztec army was to take as many prisoners as possible in a war and bring them back to Tenochtitlán. Here they were used in religious sacrifices, especially to Huizilopochtli, the god of war.

The idea of sacrifice in the name of religion was a very important part of Aztec culture. In Tenochtitlán there were several thousand priests and several different gods. These included gods of the Sun, war, wind and rain.

All of them were said to need large quantities of human blood. These human sacrifices were carried out at the top of huge, pyramid-shaped temples in an enormous square that stood right in the middle of the city.

AGRICULTURE

The Aztecs grew many different sorts of fruit on their chinampas. These included avocados, tomatoes and limes. None of these were known in Europe until they were taken there by explorers in the 16th century. The Aztecs did not have horses or wheeled vehicles, so all carrying was done by people.

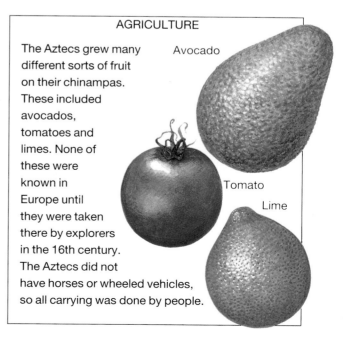

Avocado

Tomato

Lime

Arts and Crafts

In Europe, the Renaissance (*see* pages 330–333) influenced painting, sculpture and architecture, as well as education. Artists such as Titian, Holbein, Raphael, Dürer, Leonardo da Vinci, Brueghel, Botticelli and Michelangelo all worked at this time. In Britain there was a flowering in literature and drama.

In the Americas the Aztecs and Incas made ornaments in gold and silver, although they did not know how to make metal tools. Art flourished in the Ottoman, Safavid and Mogul empires and the Chinese continued to make fine porcelain.

▼ *As late as the 16th century the Incas made detailed pots from coils of clay because they had not invented the potter's wheel.*

▲ *Renaissance artists started to get proportions and perspective correct. Later on, artists painted pictures full of excitement and tension, such as Tintoretto's St George's Fight with the Dragon.*

◄ *Glazed earthenware tiles decorated the royal palace at Isfahan, Persia.*

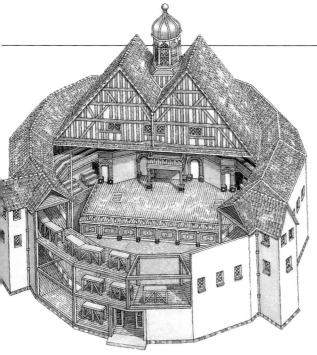

WHEN IT HAPPENED

1482 Leonardo da Vinci paints the fresco *The Last Supper* in Milan, Italy.

1508 Michelangelo Buonarroti starts work on the Sistine Chapel while the painter Raphael works on other parts of the Vatican, Rome.

1512 Albrecht Dürer, the German painter and engraver, becomes court painter to the Holy Roman emperor Maximillian I.

1536 German-born Hans Holbein becomes court painter to Henry VIII of England.

1577 The painter El Greco moves to Spain to seek the patronage of Philip II.

1586 The Kabuki theatre starts in Japan.

1600 William Shakespeare writes *Hamlet*.

▲ *Theatre-going was very popular in Elizabethan England. This is Shakespeare's Globe Theatre which was built in London in 1599.*

▼ *People who could write or play music were admired during the Renaissance. Organs and harpsicords were popular instruments.*

▶ *During the Renaissance, more realistic statues were made. When Michelangelo carved this statue of Moses in about 1513, he included veins and muscles in the arms and legs.*

1465 England: Henry VI is captured and imprisoned in the Tower of London by Edward IV. Henry's wife and son escape to Scotland and later go to France. France: The dukes of Alençon, Berri, Burgundy, Bourbon and Lorraine conspire against Louis XI, who had been attempting to limit their power. Italy: The first printing press is set up.

1466 Poland: Following the Peace of Thorn, Poland gains much of Prussia from the Teutonic Knights. England: The Earl of Warwick starts to quarrel with Edward IV. Later in the year, Warwick forms an alliance with Louis XI of France against Edward. South America: The Chimu empire is overrun by the Incas under the leadership of Topa.

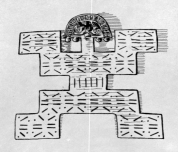

A golden pectoral ornament (worn on the chest) made by the people of South America.

1467 Charles the Bold becomes the duke of Burgundy at the age of 34. His duchy is split into two parts and includes Artois, Flanders and Brabant (which are now in Belgium) and land within the boundaries of France. His ambition is to take control of the land between the two parts of his dukedom and make himself a king. This leads to almost continual war with Louis XI of France, who is his overlord. Japan:
A period of civil war begins between the feudal lords, as each fights for control of the emperor and the country. It lasts for more than 100 years.

1468 Margaret of York, sister of Edward IV, marries Charles the Bold, Duke of Burgundy. West Africa: Sonni Ali captures Timbuktu.

The Inca Empire

The ruler of the Inca empire was known as the *Sapa Inca*. He claimed to be descended from the Sun god, who gave him the right to rule. He was also worshipped as a god himself.

Under the Sapa Inca, many officials were responsible for the everyday running of the country. They looked after the affairs of the cities and made sure the farms were working efficiently. These officials were also responsible for the factories and workshops which produced pottery, textiles and decorative metal objects. Writing was unknown to them, so they kept all their records on *quipus*. These were thick cords of different colours that had knots tied in them to convey information.

When Pachacuti became Sapa Inca (*see* pages 278–279), he began to expand his empire from the capital city Cuzco. In

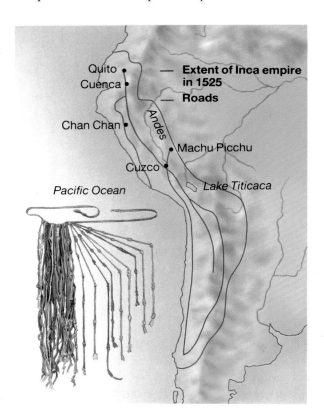

Quito
Cuenca
Extent of Inca empire in 1525
Roads
Chan Chan
Andes
Machu Picchu
Cuzco
Pacific Ocean
Lake Titicaca

▲ The ruins of the Inca city of Machu Picchu still stand high in the Andes to this day. Its temples, palaces and houses were built of granite blocks, cleverly fitted together without the use of mortar.

1450 he conquered the Titicaca basin, and in 1463 he went to war against the Lupaca and Colla tribes. In the same year he handed control of the army over to his son, Topa. Under Topa's command, the Inca army completely defeated the neighbouring Chimu empire in 1466.

Topa continued to expand the empire after he became tenth Sapa Inca in 1471. During the next 15 years he conquered land as far south as the Maule River, and he later took control of lands to the north and west. Topa also began a period of extensive road-building. Topa's son, Huayna Capac, succeeded as Sapa Inca in 1493. He also expanded the empire and built a second capital at Quito. When Huayna Capac died in 1525, the empire was divided between his sons. Huascar ruled the south and Atahualpa, the north. This division soon led to civil war.

◀ By 1525, the Inca empire was at its height. Stretching from the Andes to the coast, it measured 4000 kilometres from north to south. It had many different landscapes and climates. There were deserts near the coast and high mountains in the east.

▶ Two main roads ran north and south in the Inca empire. They were connected to every town and village by smaller roads. Goods were carried by llamas. Quipus were delivered by relay runners.

Ferdinand and Isabella

In the 15th century, Spain was divided into four different kingdoms. The two biggest were Castile and Aragon. The first step towards uniting Spain was made in 1469 when Ferdinand, heir to the King of Aragon, married Isabella, the half-sister of the King of Castile. When the king of Castile died in 1474, Isabella and Ferdinand succeeded him as joint rulers of his kingdom. Five years later, Ferdinand inherited Aragon and made Isabella joint ruler of Aragon as well.

With the two kingdoms united, Spain grew more powerful. Both Ferdinand and Isabella were devout Catholics and the Inquisition was established under their rule. It was a religious court which punished people who did not accept the Catholic Church's teachings. It operated with great severity; people were tried in secret and tortured until they confessed. Those who did confess could be fined, while those who refused were either imprisoned or burned to death.

At this time, there were many Jews

FERDINAND

1452 Born.
1469 Marries Princess Isabella of Castile.
1478 Establishes the Inquisition.
1479 Succeeds to throne of Aragon.
1481 Rules Aragon and Castile.
1492–1512 Conquers Granada, Naples and Navarre.
1516 Dies.

ISABELLA

1451 Born.
1469 Marries.
1474–1479 Campaigns for the throne of Castile.
1481 Rules Aragon and Castile jointly with Ferdinand.
1492 Finances the expedition of explorer Christopher Columbus to go to the Americas.
1504 Dies.

▼ *The army of Ferdinand and Isabella defeated the Moors in 1492. Granada became part of the kingdom of Spain and the Muslim Moors were expelled. Many of them went to live in North Africa.*

▼ *After uniting Castile and Aragon, Ferdinand and Isabella added Granada to their lands in 1492. Then Ferdinand conquered south Navarre in 1512.*

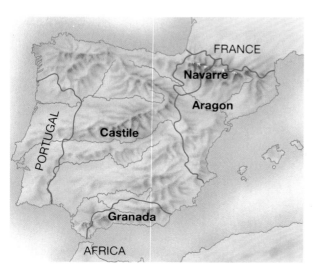

living in Spain and the Inquisition was used mainly against them. In 1492 200,000 of them were expelled from Spain. In the same year, the Moorish state of Granada was recaptured and Isabella sponsored the explorer Christopher Columbus's voyage to the Americas (*see* pages 340–341).

Ferdinand and Isabella had five children. One was Catherine of Aragon who married Henry VIII of England. But they had no son and so descent passed through their daughter Joanna the Mad.

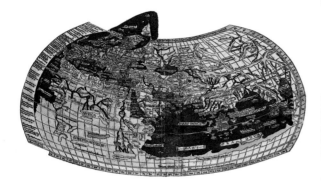

▲ *Maps at this time were based on those of Ptolemy, a 2nd century Greek mapmaker. Made in 1486 this map shows the limit of European knowledge; only half the globe is shown and Africa is joined to South-East Asia.*

1469 Spain: The marriage of Ferdinand of Aragon and Isabella of Castile leads to the unification of Spain. Italy: Lorenzo de Medici becomes joint ruler (with his brother Guiliano) of Florence at the age of 20. England: Encouraged by Louis XI and Margaret, wife of Henry VI, the Earl of Warwick and the Duke of Clarence plan a rebellion against Edward IV.

Columbus' banner bore a green cross and the symbols of Ferdinand and Isabella.

1470 England: Having changed his allegiance and joined the Lancastrians, Warwick returns to England. Edward IV flees abroad and Henry VI is restored to the throne. Ottoman empire: The Ottoman Turks seize the Greek island of Negropont (Enboea) from the Venetians.

1471 South America: Topa becomes the tenth Sapa Inca and starts on a programme of road-building to connect all parts of his vast empire with the capital, Cuzco. England: Edward IV returns to England. At the battle of Barnet he defeats and kills Warwick. He then marches west to Tewkesbury where Henry VI's wife and their son Edward, Prince of Wales, have just arrived from France. Edward IV defeats their army and captures the queen. The Prince of Wales is killed in the battle. Henry VI dies, probably murdered, in the Tower of London. Edward IV is once more King of England (to 1483). Papal States: Sixtus IV becomes pope (to 1484). Central Europe: Vladislav of Poland is elected king of Bohemia following the death of Podiebrad. North Africa: The Portuguese, led by Alfonso V, take Tangier from the Muslims. Asia: The Annamese of Vietnam begin to move southwards and conquer the Champa.

The Renaissance

In medieval Europe, the Church was the main sponsor of the arts and the main centre of education. This meant that all learning, art and sculpture had a strong religious theme. People had to accept what they were told and not ask questions. Then, in the late 14th century, Italian scholars began to take an interest in the writings of the ancient Greeks and Romans. This grew when in 1397 Manuel Chrysoloras, a scholar from Constantinople, became the first professor of Greek at the University of Florence in northern Italy.

His scholars found that works which were written before the birth of Jesus dealt with questions not answered by the Church. From this came the belief called *humanism* which says that people, and not God, control their own lives. After

▼ A street scene in Florence, one of the great centres of Renaissance learning and art. Florence grew rich on trade and commerce. Its people wore fine clothes and its streets were thronged with skilled craftsmen.

▲ During the Renaissance, architecture returned to the elegant, classical lines of ancient Greece as shown in this monument called the Tempietto, built in Rome to mark the probable spot of St Peter's crucifixion.

THE AGE OF LEARNING

In the Renaissance, the ideal person was the 'Universal Man or Woman'. This was someone who was educated to be skilful in a wide range of subjects. These included science, travel, music and literature, as well as philosophy and the arts.

The best example of a 'Universal Man' was Leonardo da Vinci. He excelled at painting, drawing, architecture and sculpture. Leonardo was also a competent engineer, musician and inventor. He trained in Florence under Verrocchio and later worked in Milan, Rome and Cloux in France. Some of his notebooks still survive. They show he was also interested in anatomy, botany and geology.

the Byzantine empire fell in 1453, still more scholars came to Italy, bringing many old manuscripts with them.

This revived interest in learning led to the period later being called the Renaissance, which means rebirth. But the Renaissance soon meant much more than simply studying the work of ancient scholars. It affected art and science, architecture and sculpture. Paintings became more realistic and no longer concentrated only on religious topics. Statues, too, were made to look like real people and some were cast in bronze for the first time since the Roman era. Rich families, such as the Medicis and the Borgias became patrons of the arts. The development of printing helped to spread the new ideas throughout Europe.

1472 Russia: Ivan III of Muscovy marries Zoë Palaeologus, the niece of the last Byzantine emperor. He adopts the Byzantine emblem of a double-headed eagle as his own. Ottoman empire: The Venetians destroy the Ottoman port of Smyrna, now known as Izmir, Turkey. At  the battle of Otluk-beli, the Turks, led by Mohammed II, defeat the Persian ruler, Uzan Hasan, who is the chief ally of the Venetians. West Africa: The Portuguese reach Fernando Po, an island off present-day Cameroon.

1473 Papal States: The Sistine Chapel is built by Giovanni de Dolci. It is the main chapel of the Vatican and is named after Pope Sixtus IV, for whom it was built.

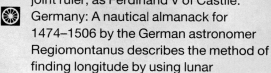

Frescoes (wall paintings) were popular in Italy. The word is from the Italian for 'fresh' because the artist painted onto wet plaster.

1474 Europe: Louis XI goes to war against Charles the Bold, Duke of Burgundy, who forms an alliance with Edward IV of England. Charles also goes to war against the Swiss Confederation. Italy: A triple alliance of the city-states of Florence, Venice and Milan is formed. Spain: Isabella succeeds to the throne of Castile. Her husband Ferdinand is made joint ruler, as Ferdinand V of Castile. Germany: A nautical almanack for 1474–1506 by the German astronomer Regiomontanus describes the method of finding longitude by using lunar distances.

1475 France: Edward IV of England invades. Later the Peace of Picquigny is signed between the two countries. By this agreement, Louis XI pays money to Edward IV to persuade him to stay in England and not pursue his claim to the throne of France. Ottoman empire: The Ottoman Turks conquer the Crimea. Italy: Birth of Michelangelo (dies 1564).

1476 England: William Caxton sets up his printing press at Westminster. He is the first printer in England and produces a varied list of books. They include Chaucer's *Canterbury Tales* (in 1478) and *The Myrrour of the World*, which is an encyclopedia and the first illustrated book to be printed in England. Switzerland: Charles the Bold occupies Granson on Lake Neuchâtel and hangs the Swiss garrison. Bern and its allies then force Charles and his army out of Granson and later out of Morat.

This elaborate salt cellar was made c. 1540 by the Italian sculptor Benvenuto Cellini for King Francis I of Spain. It is made of gold, enamel and ebony. Cellini was influenced by Michelangelo and besides being a sculptor was also a goldsmith, musician and soldier.

1477 France: In January Charles the Bold is defeated and killed at Nancy in Lorraine by the armies of the Swiss Confederation. Low Countries: In Flanders, Maximilian, son of the Holy Roman emperor Frederick III, marries Charles the Bold's daughter, Mary.

▲ *Renaissance artists began to show perspective in their paintings. Here Masolino's* King Herod's Banquet *shows objects becoming smaller with distance.*

By the 16th century, the Renaissance was at its height. As well as being interested in the distant past, people looked closely at the world about them. Instead of just accepting the teachings of the Church, they began to make detailed scientific observations for themselves.

Some studied plants and animals. Others investigated geology and astronomy. Sometimes their findings brought them into conflict with the Church. When Nicolas Copernicus (1473–1543) realized that the Earth moved round the Sun, he dared not publish his views until he was on his deathbed. He feared punishment from the Church which said that the Earth was the centre of the Universe.

This new spirit of enquiry and interest in humanity eventually led some people to question the authority of the Church and ask for change. It also led to advances in science and art, and even led some people to set sail for unexplored lands.

▶ *The rich enjoyed life at this time. Many had country villas which they visited with friends. Hunting, telling stories and making up poems were popular pastimes.*

► *Botticelli painted* La Primavera, *or* Spring, *for the Medici family between 1477 and 1478. The Greek goddess Venus, in the centre, represents love, beauty and learning.*

▼ *Leonardo's notebooks show he was interested in flight. He designed machines called ornithopters, which he thought would carry people through the air if they flapped their wings like birds do.*

Buildings

In Europe the nobility started building themselves comfortable palaces and stately homes, instead of the heavily fortified castles of the Middle Ages. More glass was available and so windows became larger. In England some houses such as Hampton Court were built of hand-made bricks, but many were still made largely of timber. This could be a fire hazard in towns where narrow streets allowed flames to spread quickly. Inside the houses, furniture was made from wood and often highly carved. Walls were often panelled with wood and ceilings were decorated with plaster. Formal gardens were laid out at this time. Especially popular were herb gardens which provided flavourings for foods and cures for simple ailments.

▲ *By the 16th century, many English town houses were built up to five storeys high. In the houses of the rich, windows were made up of many small panes of glass and the timber was often elaborately carved. This house has been made to look like the stern (rear end) of a galleon.*

TIMBER JOINTS

The strength of a timber-framed building was in the joints between the timbers. If these were made correctly, the building would hold together even if it was pushed over (as long as the timbers themselves did not break). The most-used joints were mortice and tenon, and dovetail.

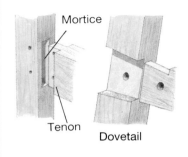

Mortice

Tenon

Dovetail

▼ *In France the castles of the Middle Ages were replaced by chateaux or manor houses. Influenced by the Renaissance, they were decorated with classical Roman designs. This staircase at Fontainebleau is a typical example.*

WHEN IT HAPPENED

1515 Henry VIII's Chancellor, Thomas Wolsey, starts building Hampton Court.

1547 Michelangelo becomes chief architect for St Peter's in Rome and designs its dome.

1569 Akbar founds a new Mogul capital at Fatehpur Sikri. Its buildings are a mixture of Muslim and Hindu architecture.

1584 Philip II's palace of El Escorial is completed near Madrid.

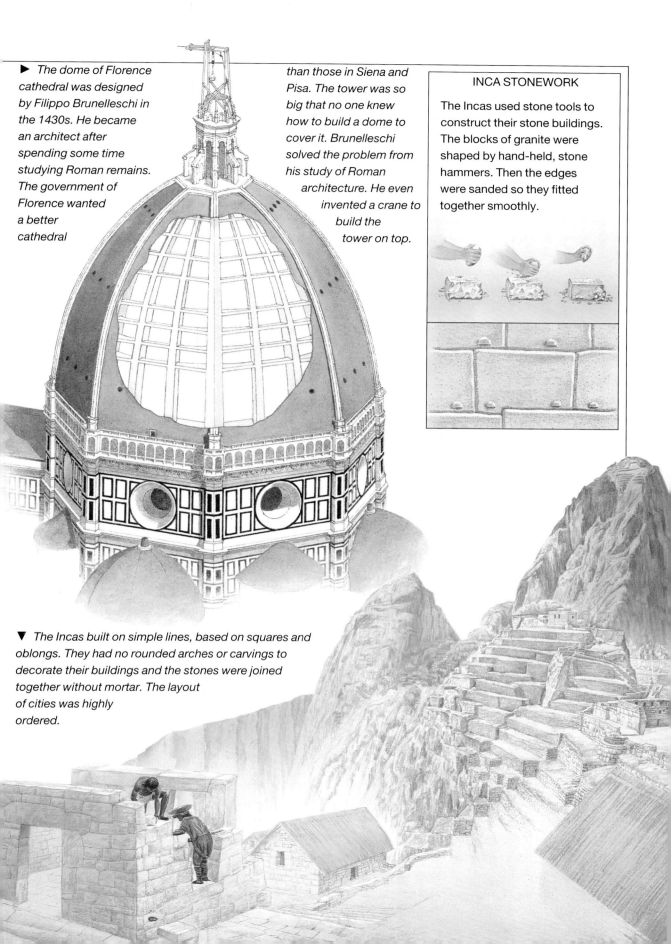

► The dome of Florence cathedral was designed by Filippo Brunelleschi in the 1430s. He became an architect after spending some time studying Roman remains. The government of Florence wanted a better cathedral than those in Siena and Pisa. The tower was so big that no one knew how to build a dome to cover it. Brunelleschi solved the problem from his study of Roman architecture. He even invented a crane to build the tower on top.

INCA STONEWORK

The Incas used stone tools to construct their stone buildings. The blocks of granite were shaped by hand-held, stone hammers. Then the edges were sanded so they fitted together smoothly.

▼ The Incas built on simple lines, based on squares and oblongs. They had no rounded arches or carvings to decorate their buildings and the stones were joined together without mortar. The layout of cities was highly ordered.

1478 England: Edward IV of England has his brother, the Duke of Clarence, executed. Spain: Ferdinand and Isabella establish the Spanish Inquisition with the consent of Pope Sixtus IV. At this time it is mainly used to punish so-called 'converted' Jews who live in Spain and still practise their old faith in secret. They are burned at the stake or condemned to prison. Italy: Lorenzo de Medici becomes sole ruler of Florence (to 1492) after his brother Giuliano de Medici is assassinated. Russia: Ivan III conquers Novgorod and makes it part of the duchy of Moscow. Eastern Europe: Hungary gains Moravia and Silesia. Ottoman empire: The Ottoman Turks conquer Albania.

1479 Spain: Ferdinand, also known as the Catholic king, succeeds to the throne of Aragon as Ferdinand II. His wife Isabella becomes joint ruler with him. Spain is united by this formal union of Aragon and Castile. Eastern Europe: In the Treaty of Constantinople, Venice agrees to pay tribute to the Ottoman empire for trading rights in the Black Sea.

A coin bearing the head of Cosimo de Medici, Lorenzo de Medici's grandfather.

1480 Russia: Ivan III ends Muscovy's allegiance to the Tartars (the Golden Horde) who have controlled Russia for over 250 years. Mediterranean: Ottoman Turks besiege the island of Rhodes, held by the Knights of St John.

1481 Ottoman empire: Muhammad II, the great Ottoman ruler, dies at the age of 51. He is also known as Muhammad the Conqueror, after his defeat of the Byzantine empire in 1453.

Italy

At this time Italy was divided into small states. Many of them were large cities, such as Florence, Venice and Rome. Others were ducal courts such as Mantua, Urbino and Ferrara. Most of these states were ruled by families who had grown rich on trade and commerce in the late Middle Ages.

The most powerful family of the day was the Medicis of Florence who had made a great fortune in the 14th century through banking and moneylending. The best-known is Lorenzo, who became joint ruler of Florence with his brother in 1469. He was a clever statesman and also a patron of writers, artists and scientists. He was keen to promote his family and saw his second son become pope. Under his influence, Florence became one of the most beautiful and prosperous cities in Italy, as well as a centre of the

LORENZO DE MEDICI

Lorenzo (1449–1492) became joint ruler of Florence at the age of 20. When his brother died, he took the title *Magnifico Signore* and was known as Lorenzo the Magnificent. He made Florence the leading state in Italy. He was a great patron of literature and art.

LUCRETIA BORGIA

Lucretia (1480–1519), Pope Alexander VI's daughter, was married four times to further her father's ambition. Two were annulled (cancelled) and her brother killed one husband. Despite this, her court at Ferrara was a centre for artists, poets and scholars.

Renaissance. Lorenzo had a large art collection of his own and, through his writings, helped to make the form of Italian spoken in Florence into the language of the whole country.

Another famous family was the Borgias. In 1455 Alfonso Borgia became Pope Calistus III. His nephew, Rodrigo, was later made Pope Alexander VI. He had many illegitimate childen and wanted them all to be rich and powerful, but, on his death, the family's power collapsed. In contrast to the Borgias, Federigo, Duke of Urbino, spent much of his money on building churches, schools and hospitals. Like Lorenzo de Medici, he was interested in the arts and had a famous library built in his palace. Federigo was popular with his subjects and did not need a bodyguard, unlike any other Italian ruler of that time.

▲ During the Middle Ages much of Italy was controlled by the Holy Roman Empire. A power struggle between emperors and popes left them both weakened. Italian cities formed their own independent states. In the 16th century Italy came under attack from Spain.

▼ The Villa Poggio was Lorenzo de Medici's country home. Wealthy men built country villas with carefully laid out gardens. Elegant houses like this gradually replaced the fortified buildings of earlier times. At the same time many Italians were extremely poor.

European Exploration

In the second half of the 15th century, European sailors and navigators began to plan voyages which would take them beyond the limits of the world they knew. This was partly a result of the new interest in the world encouraged by the Renaissance (*see* pages 330–331), but the main reason was to set up new trading links with the spice-producing countries of Asia.

Until the Byzantine empire fell in 1453, spices were brought overland to Constantinople and then taken across the Mediterranean to the countries of Europe. This made them expensive.

In spite of this, spices were an essential part of everyday life. There was no refrigeration so the only way to preserve meat was by salting it. Adding spices helped to hide the salty taste, and they also concealed the taste of meat which had gone bad despite being salted.

After 1453, direct land links between Europe and Asia were cut completely. If

DIAS

In 1486 Bartholomeu Dias (1450–1500) was given the command of three ships to explore the coast of Africa. Strong gales blew him round the Cape of Good Hope, but he turned back as his crew were unwilling to go any further. He drowned near the Cape in 1500.

DA GAMA

After rounding the Cape of Good Hope in 1497, Vasco da Gama (1469–1525) sailed up the east coast of Africa and with the help of an Indian sailor crossed the ocean to Calicut in India. He returned home with a cargo of spices. He returned to India in 1502 and again in 1522.

▼ *Vasco da Gama's small ships were a development on the caravel and its triangular, lateen sail. They had both square and lateen rigged sails which made them a great deal more manoeuvrable on the open sea.*

NAVIGATIONAL INSTRUMENTS

Navigation at sea was very primitive at this time. The only instruments which were available were the compass, the astrolabe and the backstaff.

The compass was the most important navigational aid because it showed which direction the ship was sailing in. This was still a relatively new invention in Europe, but the Chinese had used it since the 12th century. Both the astrolabe and the backstaff used the Sun or a star to calculate a ship's latitude (how far north or south of the equator the ship was). But they were difficult to use if the sky was overcast. It was also difficult to work out how fast a ship was going and its longitude (how far east or west the ship was).

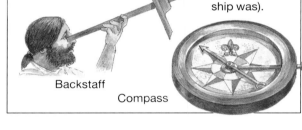

Astrolabe

Backstaff

Compass

spices were to reach Europe, then a sea route to the East had to be found. When the Portuguese began exploring the west coast of Africa in the 1460s (*see* pages 306–307) they set up forts and traded in gold, ivory and silver.

Gradually they sailed further south and Bartholomeu Dias reached the Cape of Good Hope at the tip of Africa in 1488. Ten years later, he helped Vasco da Gama to plan a voyage which took him round the Cape and across the Indian Ocean to Calicut. Da Gama was followed by Pedro Cabral who returned from India with a cargo of pepper. This encouraged other navigators to try and sail further east. In 1517 the Portuguese reached China, and nearly 30 years later they arrived in Japan. The Portuguese were not only driven by trade but also by a determination to spread Christianity.

1482 West Africa: The Portuguese navigator Diego Cao starts an exploration of the Congo River (to 1484). Portuguese traders establish settlements on the Gold Coast, now known as Ghana, where they trade for gold and ivory.

1483 England: Edward IV of England dies. His 12-year-old son becomes Edward V. Edward IV's youngest brother, Richard Duke of Gloucester, is made Protector of Edward V during his childhood. However, Richard takes the throne as Richard III. Edward V and his younger brother Richard are imprisoned in the Tower of London, where they die, probably murdered. France: Louis XI dies and Charles VIII succeeds to the throne (to 1498). Italy: Raphael, Italian painter and architect, is born (dies 1520).

1484 England: Caxton prints *Morte D'Arthur*, the poetic collection of legends about King Arthur compiled by Sir Thomas Malory. Papal States: Innocent VIII is elected pope (to 1492).

1485 England: Henry Tudor, Earl of Richmond and a descendant of Edward III, lands in England from France. He defeats and kills Richard III at the battle of Bosworth Field. Henry Tudor is then crowned as Henry VII (to 1509), the first of the Tudor monarchs. Eastern Europe: Hungary becomes the most powerful state by capturing Vienna and acquiring lower Austria. South America: The Incas under Topa conquer all of what is now Chile as far as the Maule River. They also conquer the south coast of Peru and the north-west of Argentina.

A woodcut of a blacksmith from a book published by Caxton in 1483.

1486 England: Henry VII of England marries Elizabeth of York, daughter of Edward IV, and so unites the houses of York and Lancaster. Germany: Maximilian becomes king (to 1493).

1487 West Africa: The Portuguese reach Timbuktu by travelling overland from the coast.

1488 South Africa: The Portuguese navigator, Bartholomeu Dias, rounds the Cape of Good Hope, Africa's southern-most point. Scotland: After defeating and killing his father at Sauchieburn, James IV becomes king (to 1513).

1490 Italy: Aldus Manutius sets up the Aldine Press in Venice to make more classical works available. West Africa: The Portuguese sail up the River Congo for about 320 kilometres and convert the king of the Congo to Christianity.

1492 Americas: Christopher Columbus crosses the Atlantic and arrives in the Caribbean islands, which he calls the West Indies. Spain: Ferdinand conquers Granada and ends Muslim influence in his country. The Moors and the Jews are expelled from Spain. Jews are also expelled from Sciliy and Sardinia. England: The King of France pays Henry VII £149,000 not to go to war with him. Papal States: Rodrigo Borgia is elected as Pope Alexander VI (to 1503). Germany: First modern globe is made by Martin Behaim of Nuremberg.

The world map of Henricus Martellus, published in 1490, showed advances on previous maps. It showed sea separating Africa and Asia, and mapped approximately three quarters of the globe.

While the Portuguese sailed east, the Spanish sailed west. In 1492, Queen Isabella sponsored Christopher Columbus, a navigator from Genoa in Italy, to find a route to India. Existing maps showed the world to be much smaller than it really is. When Columbus reached a group of islands across the Atlantic, he was sure he had reached his goal and called them the West Indies. In fact, they were the Caribbean Islands off the coast of North America. Columbus made three more voyages there, but he never realized his mistake.

Another Italian, Amerigo Vespucci, reached the north-east coast of South America in 1499. On a second voyage in 1501 he explored as far as the Rio de la Plata, Uruguay and realized he had found a new continent. A map in 1507 named the continent America after him.

Other Europeans tried to find a northern route to India. One was John Cabot, a Venetian who was sponsored in 1497 by Henry VIII of England, to

MAGELLAN

Ferdinand Magellan (c. 1480–1521) led the first expedition to sail round the world in 1519. The voyage took three years but he only survived as far as the Philippines. He gave the Pacific Ocean its name. The Magellan Straits in South America, are also named after him.

COLUMBUS

Christopher Columbus (1451–1506) first went to sea as a pirate. In 1476 he settled in Portugal after being shipwrecked. When the Portuguese king would not sponsor his voyage to reach India by sailing west, he asked the Spanish monarchs. They took six years to say yes.

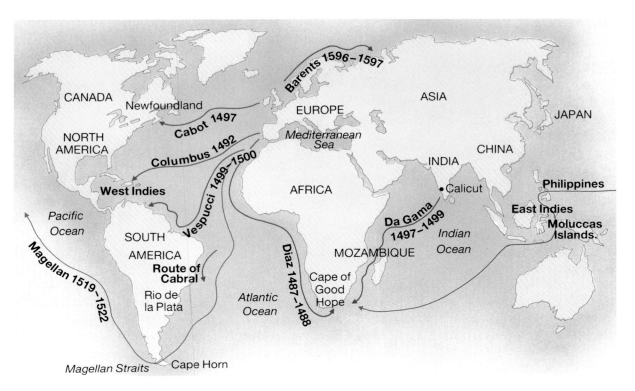

explore the northern ocean. Another explorer called Jacques Cartier sailed up Canada's St Lawrence River in 1535 and claimed land near it for France.

In August 1519 Ferdinand Magellan left Spain to find a western route to the Spice Islands (Moluccas). He crossed into the Pacific, but was killed in the Philippines. Juan Sebastian del Cano then took over, arriving back in Spain in September 1522 with just one ship.

▲ Navigators from Spain, Portugal, England and France tried many different routes to reach the spice-producing islands of the Moluccas. This widened European knowledge of the world, led to increased trade and the setting up of new empires.

▼ Columbus set sail on his voyage in a ship similar to this one. He took three ships; the flagship Santa Maria, was only 36 metres long but it was twice the size of the other two, the Pinta and the Niña. The crew had no accommodation and their food was cooked on deck.

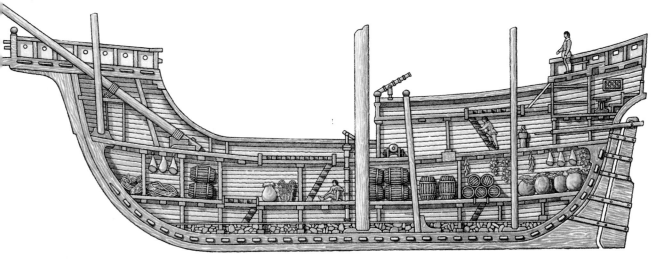

Communications

As the knowledge of printing spread through Europe, many more books were published. More people learned to read. New ideas in science and the arts reached many people at the same time and so people everywhere knew the same things. However, nothing could travel faster than the speed of a horse. Most news was passed on by word of mouth and there was no postal service as we know it today. Most roads were so badly maintained that it was often faster to travel by sea or river. When the Spanish arrived in America, they found the people knew nothing about horses or wheeled vehicles. It took weeks for messages to go to and from Europe which made government very difficult.

Mountain   Montezuma

Tree

Tenochtitlan

Teeth   Stone

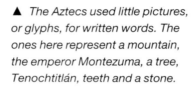

▲ *The Aztecs used little pictures, or glyphs, for written words. The ones here represent a mountain, the emperor Montezuma, a tree, Tenochtitlán, teeth and a stone.*

▲ *In 1588 a chain of beacons was set up on hill-tops in England. Each one could see the next in either direction. Their fires were lit to warn of the Spanish Armada.*

▶ *Christopher Columbus crossed the Atlantic with three small sailing ships in 1492. The journey took 30 days to complete. His ships bore the cross of Christianity.*

1476 William Caxton sets up the first printing press in England.

1500 Wynken de Worde sets up a printing press in Fleet Street, London. The street is a centre for printing for almost 500 years.

c. 1530 By now the Incas are using a code of knots tied in strings of different thicknesses.

1539 The Spaniards set up the first printing press in the Americas. It is in Mexico City.

▲ In the Inca empire, relay runners carried official messages and packages. The first set off and ran about 1.5 kilometres to a shelter. From there a second runner took the message for another 1.5 kilometres. Each runner blew on a shell to announce his approach.

▲ The publisher Aldus Manutius set up the Aldine Press in Venice in about 1490. There he produced some of the first printed copies of ancient Greek and Roman classical works. These pages are from The Dream of Poliphilus which he published in 1499.

▶ During the 15th century books were very expensive, but Lorenzo de Medici was able to collect together a great private library in Florence. In 1571 it was refounded as a public library in a building designed by Michelangelo.

1493 Americas: Pope Alexander VI divides newly discovered lands between Spain and Portugal using an imaginary Line of Demarcation. Spain can claim land to the west of it and Portugal can claim land to the east. West Africa: The Songhay empire reaches its greatest extent under Askia Muhammad who takes over much of the Mandingo empire. Holy Roman Empire: Maximilian I becomes Holy Roman emperor (to 1519). South America: Huayna Capac becomes the 11th Sapa Inca. He founds a second capital at Quito in the north of his empire.

1494 Italy: Charles VIII of France invades Italy. Inspired by Girolamo Savonarola, the people of Florence depose the Medici family. Iberian Peninsula: By the Treaty of Tordesillas, Spain and Portugal move the pope's Line of Demarcation farther west. This will eventually give Portugal territory in eastern Brazil.

1495 Italy: Charles VIII enters Naples. The Holy League, made up of Milan, Venice, Maximilian I, Pope Alexander VI and Ferdinand of Spain, forces him to withdraw.

1496 England: Henry VII of England joins the Holy League. Western Europe: A commercial treaty is drawn up between England and the Netherlands.

1497 North America: Italian-born John Cabot crosses the Atlantic and arrives in Newfoundland. He is probably the first European to go there since the Vikings, five centuries before. Africa: Vasco da Gama sails around Africa.

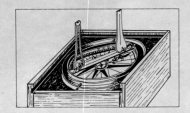

Magnetic compasses such as this one were used in the 1500s by explorers to plan their routes across unknown waters.

The Songhay Empire

When Europeans first went to Africa in the 1460s, the continent was made up of many different states and kingdoms. They had their own trade networks and practised advanced forms of farming. In some areas gold and copper were mined and in others cloth making and metal-casting were important activities.

One of the most important kingdoms was Songhay in West Africa. Tradition says that it was founded in the 7th century by a Berber Christian called al-Yaman. It later became part of the Mali empire and was a Muslim state from the 11th century onward (*see* pages 264–265). In 1464 Sonni Ali made Songhay independent again and expanded its territory, taking over what had been the Mali empire and adding to it. Writers in the city of Timbuktu described him as cruel and immoral.

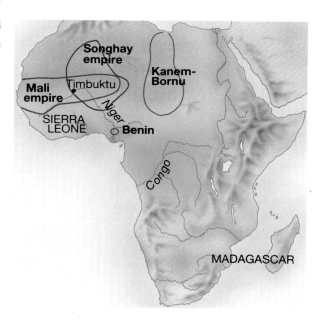

▲ *Early European explorers that settled on the coasts of Africa knew nothing about its rich interior. Songhay traded its gold and slaves for luxury goods and salt.*

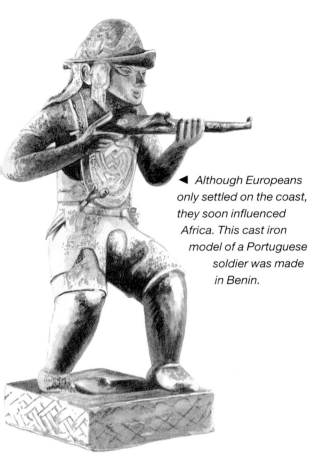

◄ *Although Europeans only settled on the coast, they soon influenced Africa. This cast iron model of a Portuguese soldier was made in Benin.*

They also said that he persecuted men of religion, while pretending to be a Muslim. When Sonni Ali died by drowning, he was succeeded by his son, Bakari. However, Bakari was weak and the al-Yaman line died out with him.

In 1493, Askia Muhammad I founded a new dynasty in Songhay and made it the most important empire in West Africa. Its wealth was built on the trading cities of Gao and Timbuktu. Here gold from the south was exchanged for salt from the north. Leo Africanus, a Spanish Muslim, visited Timbuktu in the early 16th century and wrote that the king had 'many plates and sceptres of gold'. He also noted that 'manuscripts and books...are sold for more money than any other merchandise'. Askia was followed by weak rulers, and in 1591 the Songhay empire fell to the Moroccans.

▼ *Timbuktu, first controlled by the Mali empire was taken over by the Songhay. It had a university, a mosque and more than 100 schools. Gold, ivory, cloth, salt, copper and slaves were all sold in its markets.*

KANEM-BORNU

Kanem-Bornu was an African empire which grew up around Lake Chad. Kanem became a centre of Muslim civilization in the 11th century and was situated on the eastern trade routes through Africa. When its king was expelled in 1389 he founded a new dynasty in Bornu. In the 16th century Bornu conquered Kanem. It reached its peak under Idris Aloma who came to power in 1571 and ruled till 1603.

1498 Columbus finds his way to Trinidad and the coast of South America. Huayna Capac extends his Inca empire north of Quito into what is now Colombia. The Andes highway is completed. France: Louis XII, king (to 1515). Italy: In Florence, Savonarola is burned at the stake by his political rivals. Vasco da Gama reaches India.

c.1498 Modern-style toothbrushes are being used in China.

1499 South America: Amerigo Vespucci explores the north-east coast of South America. Italy: Louis XII of France invades.

A standard from Safavid Persia. It was probably used in a religious ceremony and would have been carried in the annual procession to honour those who were killed in battle in 1080.

1500 Blown off course on his way to India, Pedro Cabral lands on the coast of Brazil and claims the country for Portugal. Italy: Louis XII conquers Milan; in the Treaty of Granada, he and Ferdinand of Spain agree to divide Naples between them.

1501 Amerigo Vespucci explores the coast of Brazil. Italy: France and Spain occupy Naples. Russia and Poland are at war (until 1503). Shah Ismail founds the Safavid dynasty in Persia (now Iran).

1502 The first Africans arrive as slaves in the Americas. Columbus lands in Nicaragua. Scotland: Margaret, daughter of Henry VII of England, marries James IV. War breaks out between France and Spain.

1503 Italy: France is defeated by Spain at the battles of Cerignola and Garigliano. Papal States: Julius II is elected pope (to 1513); he demolishes the old St Peter's and plans a new church in the Renaissance style of architecture. Italy: Leonardo da Vinci paints the *Mona Lisa*.

Safavid Persia

The Safavid dynasty came to power in Persia (now Iran) at the start of the 16th century. It was founded by Ismail I who captured the city of Tabriz in 1501 and had himself crowned *shah* or ruler. The name Safavid came from one of Ismail's ancestors called Safi od-Din who lived in the 13th century.

By 1508 Ismail controlled the whole of Persia and most of Mesopotamia (now Iraq). In contrast to the rest of the Muslim world, which followed the Sunni branch of Islam, he established Shiism as the state religion in his country. The Sunnis believed that the *caliph* or leader of Islam should be chosen by the people, the Shiites believed that only the descendants of Muhammad's family should be caliphs. These differences, together with disputes over lands, led to a long series of religious wars between the Safavids and the Ottoman empire (*see* pages 358–359). They started in 1514 when the Ottoman sultan, Selim I, invaded western Persia.

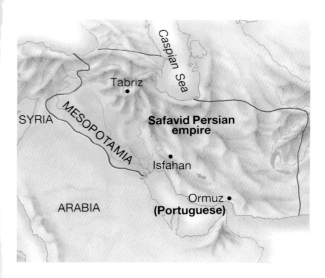

▲ *The heart of the Safavid empire was Persia. Isfahan became the capital during the long reign of Abbas I. In 1497 the Portuguese occupied the island of Ormuz.*

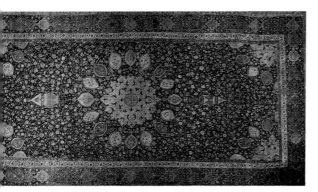

◄ Many fine carpets were made during the Safavid dynasty. They were handmade from wool which was dyed in different colours. The carpets were covered in patterns similar to ones used on pottery and tiles. This carpet was made in 1539.

ABBAS I

1557 Born.
1587 Becomes fifth Safavid shah.
1590 Ends war with the Ottoman Turks.
1598 Drives Uzbek Turks from north-eastern Persia.
1602 Goes to war with Ottoman empire.
1604 Defeats Ottomans at Tabriz.
1628 Dies.

The Safavid dynasty reached its peak under Shah Abbas I, known as the Great. A good military leader, he moved his capital to Isfahan and made it into a beautiful city, building a magnificent palace and mosque. Covered *bazaars* or shops surrounded the main square, trees and streams flanked the market square and a central avenue had gardens growing on either side of it. However, Abbas is said to have had his children blinded because he feared them as rivals.

▼ Part of the mosque at Isfahan built by Abbas the Great in honour of his father-in-law. It is decorated with patterns based on geometric designs and plant shapes. Some of the patterns are carved into the stone, but most of them are painted on to ceramic tiles.

Food and Farming

When Europeans arrived in the Americas they found many foods they had never seen before, such as potatoes, tomatoes, new varieties of beans, pineapples and bananas. They brought some back to Europe and found that many would grow there too.

Europe still had famines when the harvest failed. It was still not possible to feed all the animals over the winter and so many were killed in the autumn. The population, however, was increasing so more marshland was reclaimed for farming, especially in England and the Netherlands.

▲ An early drawing of a pineapple. It was one of the fruits Columbus discovered in the West Indies.

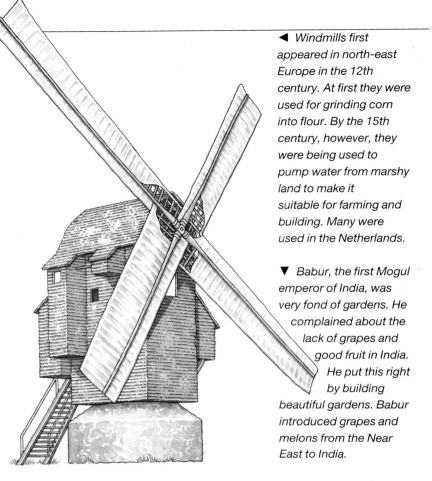

◄ Windmills first appeared in north-east Europe in the 12th century. At first they were used for grinding corn into flour. By the 15th century, however, they were being used to pump water from marshy land to make it suitable for farming and building. Many were used in the Netherlands.

▼ Babur, the first Mogul emperor of India, was very fond of gardens. He complained about the lack of grapes and good fruit in India. He put this right by building beautiful gardens. Babur introduced grapes and melons from the Near East to India.

◀ Some of the Native Americans in Virginia lived by growing corn and hunting. So that the corn did not all ripen at once, they planted three crops of it each year.

▲ By now the feudal system had almost disappeared from Europe. Everyone still worked together at harvest, however, as this 16th century Dutch painting shows.

▶ To grow crops, the Incas had to cut terraces in the steep slopes of the Andes. They then harvested the crop with a wooden digging-stick, called a taclla. On the high ground llamas and alpacas grazed. Both men and women worked in the fields.

WHEN IT HAPPENED

1492 At the time of Columbus' arrival, Caribbean Arawaks grow yams, cotton and tobacco.

1512 The Portuguese start trading in the spices cloves and nutmeg from the Moluccas.

1534 To stop landlords evicting tenants, Henry VIII bans flocks of more than 2000 sheep.

1570s After a slave revolt on Sâo Tomé, off the coast of West Africa, the Portuguese set up sugar plantations in Brazil.

1504 Central Asia: Babur captures Kabul in Afghanistan. It will later be the base from which he sets out to capture northern India and founds the Mogul dynasty. Germany: The watch  is invented by Peter Henlein of Nuremberg. It only has a single hand.

1505 Italy: By the Treaty of Blois, France keeps Milan but cedes Naples to Spain. This gives Spain control of southern Italy. East Africa: The Portuguese establish trading posts on the Malabar coast and found Mozambique. Russia: Basil III, son of Ivan III, becomes ruler of Moscow.

1506 Spain: Columbus dies in poverty, still convinced that the lands he has visited are part of Asia.

1507 Germany: Martin Waldseemuller produces a world map. It is the first to show South America as separate from Asia and uses the name America, named after Amerigo Vespucci.

The great seal of Henry VIII.

1508 Europe: In the League of Cambrai, the Holy Roman emperor Maximilian I, Louis of France and Ferdinand of Spain ally against Venice. Papal States: Michelangelo starts painting the Sistine Chapel in the Vatican. The artist Raphael (Raphaello Sanzio) also begins work on decorating the Vatican for the pope.

1509 England: Henry VII dies and is succeeded by his 17-year-old son, Henry VIII (to 1547). South-East Asia: Victory at the battle of Diu establishes Portuguese control of Indian Ocean.

The Early Tudors

When Henry Tudor became Henry VII of England in 1485 (*see* page 316) he started a dynasty which ruled until 1603. Henry strengthened his position by banning private armies. He also executed and took estates from any lord who opposed him. Henry's policies of harsh taxation and careful spending also increased the wealth of the Crown. In 1492 Henry even persuaded the French king to pay him money each year for not going to war against France.

When Henry VIII came to the throne in 1509, England was an important power in Europe. Henry married Catherine of Aragon, the daughter of Ferdinand and Isabella of Spain. He went to war successfully against France in 1513, and in the same year defeated the Scots at Flodden and killed their king.

HENRY VIII

1491 Born.
1509 Becomes king.
1521 Supports the pope against Martin Luther; is made 'Defender of the Faith'.
1534 Severs English Church from papal authority and becomes head of the Church of England.
1536 Closes many monasteries.
1547 Dies.

HENRY'S WIVES

Henry married six times. He divorced two of his wives and had two more executed. After divorcing Catherine of Aragon, he married Anne Boleyn. She gave birth to Elizabeth but was beheaded in 1536. Only his third wife, Jane Seymour, provided him with a son, Edward. Jane died in 1537. Henry divorced Anne of Cleves after six months of marriage, and beheaded Catherine Howard, but Catherine Parr survived him.

THE MARY ROSE

Henry VIII was always at war with the French, so he strengthened the English navy. His pride and joy was a ship called the *Mary Rose*. After it had been refitted in 1536, Henry and his court went to watch it sail on the Solent. Some 700 sailors, soldiers and archers stood on the deck. This affected the ship's balance so much that, when a gust of wind blew, it capsized and quickly sank.

Although Catherine of Aragon had five or six children, they all died except Princess Mary. As Henry wanted a son to make the Tudor dynasty secure, he decided to divorce Catherine and marry again. To do this he needed the pope's permission. The pope refused to agree so, with the help of Thomas Cromwell his chief minister and Thomas Cranmer then Archbishop of Canterbury, he broke from the Roman Catholic Church and made himself supreme head of the Church in England. This new Church granted him a divorce and he married Anne Boleyn in 1533. Three years later Henry began to close the monasteries and nunneries in England and Wales. He sold most of their land to help pay for wars against France.

▼ *Sir Thomas More, shown here with his family, was Lord Chancellor from 1529 to 1532. He resigned when Henry broke away from the Catholic Church and he was executed for treason in 1535.*

The Portuguese Empire

When the Portuguese explorers reached the East Indies in the early 16th century, they found that these islands were rich in the spices that Europe wanted. To control this valuable trade, the Portuguese conquered the Moluccas Islands and seized the main ports in the Indian Ocean. As Portuguese traders had to sail around the Cape of Good Hope to return to Lisbon, forts were set up at various places along the coast of Africa to protect them. From Africa, the Portuguese took gold and also slaves to work on the sugar plantations.

At first they had plantations on the African island of Sâo Tomé. When the slaves there revolted in the 1570s, the Portuguese set up sugar plantations in Brazil. A large part of this country was in their empire and the African slaves were taken to work there instead.

▶ This ivory carving from West Africa shows Portuguese soldiers standing in a miniature crow's nest on a ship. It dates from the 16th century.

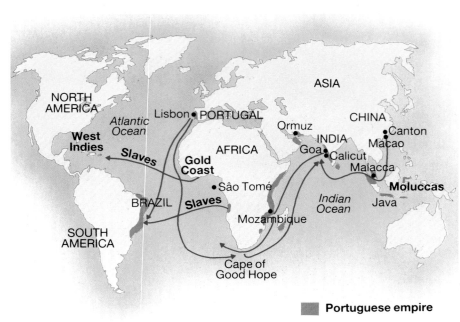

◀ The Portuguese empire at its greatest extent in about 1600. As well as trading, the Portuguese tried to spread Christianity. Missionaries had little influence in the East where there was no colonization beyond the trading-posts, but they were much more successful in Brazil. The Portuguese monopoly on spices ended after 1600 when England and the Netherlands set up East India companies to trade in spices for themselves.

▲ *An ivory carving made in 1540 shows a Portuguese nobleman and his wife at the dinner table. Many Portuguese grew rich on trade. In Brazil and India they lived in splendour, surrounded by many servants.*

At its height in the 16th century, the Portuguese empire also included the islands of Cape Verde, Madeira and the Azores, and narrow strips of land on the east and west coasts of Africa. The Portuguese occupied long stretches of Angola and Mozambique, the bases of Ormuz, Goa, Calicut and Colombo in the Indian Ocean, and trading posts in the Far East, such as Macao in China, the Celebes, Java and Malacca.

▲ *Before the Portuguese arrived in the Moluccas its rulers enjoyed the profit from the lucrative spice trade. But under Portuguese rule local people were forced to harvest cloves and nutmeg for them. Other spices from the East included pepper, cinnamon and ginger.*

1510 Italy: Pope Julius II and Venice form a Holy League to drive Louis XII of France from Italy. Europe: Sunflowers are introduced to Europe from America.

1511 Europe: Ferdinand of Spain and Henry VIII of England join the Holy League against France.

1512 Italy: The Swiss join the Holy League and drive the French from Milan. Eastern Europe: Russia is at war with Poland (to 1522). Ottoman empire: Selim I becomes sultan (to 1520).

1513 Vasco Nuñez de Balboa reaches the Pacific. Scotland: James IV of Scotland is killed at the battle of Flodden Field. His son becomes James V (to 1542). Italy: At the battle of Novara the French are defeated and driven out of Italy. Papal States: Giovanni de Medici is elected Pope Leo X (to 1521).

1514 France: Mary, sister of Henry VIII, marries Louis XII of France. Near East: War breaks out between the Ottoman and Safavid empires. The Ottoman Turks win the battle of Chaldiran.

This collar was designed to stop African slaves from lying down or escaping.

1515 England: Thomas Wolsey is made Lord Chancellor of England and a cardinal. France: Louis XII dies and Francis I becomes king of France (to 1547). Italy: At the battle of Marignano, the French defeat the Swiss and regain Milan.

1516 Europe: In the Treaty of Noyon France gives up its claim to Naples. Spain: Ferdinand of Spain dies. His grandson becomes Charles I (to 1556). Ottoman empire: War breaks out with Egypt; Selim I defeats the Egyptians at the battle of Marjdabik. Europe: Coffee is first introduced.

The Reformation

By the early 16th century, the new ideas of the Renaissance led some people to challenge the teachings of the Roman Catholic Church. At the same time, the way its leaders ran the Church was strongly criticized. Many monks and nuns no longer led lives of poverty, while some popes and bishops thought more about money and power than religion. People felt the Church should be reformed.

The movement which started this was called the Reformation. It began in Germany in 1517 when a priest called Martin Luther nailed a list of 95 statements to the church door at Wittenberg. It gave details of all he thought was wrong with the Church. Most of all Luther hated the Church's sale of Indulgences. These certificates forgave people their sins, and could be bought from the Church for money.

LUTHER

Martin Luther (c. 1483 –1546) believed that man was saved by faith alone, not by good works or by the sale of Indulgences. He wanted faith to be based on scriptures in the Bible and not on religious ceremonies. He also believed Bible reading was important and that services should be in the local language, not Latin.

CALVIN

John Calvin (1509– 1564), born in France, was originally named Jean Chauvin. He studied law and theology, before becoming involved in the Reformation. He believed in predestination (that God had already ordained the future) and that only people chosen by God, the Elect, would be saved.

▶ The Protestant faith had become the main religion of Sweden and Finland by 1529. In 1536 it was adopted in Denmark and Norway. The seven northern provinces of the Netherlands followed the teachings of Calvin, but they were ruled by the Catholic king of Spain who tried to suppress the new religion. Most of Scotland became Protestant, as did England and Wales, but Ireland and southern Europe stayed Catholic. Divisions between the two religions in France later led to civil war.

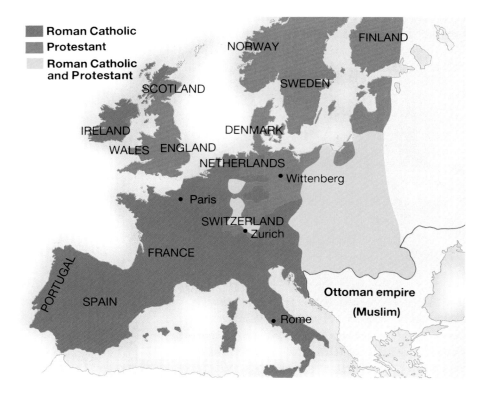

Roman Catholic
Protestant
Roman Catholic and Protestant

▲ *The sale of Indulgences, shown in this illustration based on a Protestant woodcut of the time, was used to raise money for the Roman Catholic Church.*

Luther hoped his list would lead to debate in the Church, but instead he was accused of heresy (going against Church beliefs). He refused to take back his words and he was excommunicated (excluded) from the Catholic Church in 1521. By this time, Luther had gained support in northern Germany and in Switzerland. He set up his own church and his followers were called Lutherans. After 1529 they were renamed Protestants when they protested against attempts to limit their teachings.

Ulrich Zwingli led the Reformation in Switzerland. His views were more extreme than Luther's. In 1524 he banned Catholic mass in Zurich. This led to a civil war in which Zwingli was killed. Zwingli was followed by John Calvin. He completed the Reformation in Switzerland and influenced John Knox who took the Reformation to Scotland.

1517 Germany: The Reformation begins when Martin Luther protests about corruption in the Church. He is especially concerned about the sale of Indulgences to raise money for a new St Peter's church in Rome. Ottoman empire: The Mameluke empire collapses when the Ottoman Turks capture Cairo. Syria and Egypt are added to the Ottoman empire. China: The Portuguese reach Canton.

1518 Italy: Forks are first used at a banquet in Venice. Germany: The first fire engine is constructed by Anthony Blatner.

1519 Switzerland: Ulrich Zwingli leads the Reformation in Switzerland. Holy Roman Empire: Charles I of Spain becomes Holy Roman Emperor Charles V (to 1556), after his grandfather, Maximilian I, dies. Spain: Ferdinand Magellan sets out to circumnavigate the world.

1520 France: At the Field of the Cloth of Gold, Francis I of France meets Henry VIII of England but fails to gain the latter's support against Charles V, the Holy Roman Emperor. Instead, Henry makes a secret treaty with Charles. Ottoman empire: Suleiman I, also known as the Magnificent and the Lawgiver, becomes sultan (to 1566). Europe: Chocolate is introduced.

A woodcut illustration for The Art of Dying Well, *published in Germany in about 1470 and used by the Church as a sermon in pictures.*

People

By 1500 the population of Europe had grown again to the size it had been before the Black Death in the 14th century. Most people still lived in the country, but there was no longer enough land for everybody. Many people moved into towns. Some found jobs, but others became beggars. By 1600 some Europeans lived in colonies overseas.

While the ideas of the Renaissance affected the lives of the rich, many poorer people were more concerned with just staying alive. It was a time when plagues still killed thousands and lack of food meant diseases such as influenza had high death rates. In spite of this, people still enjoyed street entertainments and going to see plays.

▲ *This selection of items from the ship* Mary Rose *shows what a sailor was likely to take to sea in 1536. They include a pouch, a whistle, a comb and a rosary.*

Whistle

Rosary

Comb

Pocket sundial

▼ *European children played many different games. These included leap-frog, tag, follow-my-leader and rolling bowls or hoops.*

▶ *The Native North Americans of the Eastern Woodlands wore moccasins made from a single piece of leather. On the Great Plains they made wooden pipes for smoking tobacco and decorated them with colourful woven cloth.*

◀ Many children died young, and so people often had large families in the hope that some would survive to be adults. This church memorial records the 24 children born to a woman in Cornwall.

◀ This couple are wearing clothes which were fashionable at court in Europe around 1570. The men usually wore plainer colours than the women, but their doublets were often encrusted with jewels. Most rich women wore luxury fabrics such as velvet, brocade, silk and lace.

▼ In most countries sons were thought to be more important than daughters. Some dynasties died out because there was no son to continue the line. The birth of a son to a popular ruler was often the cause for a celebration, as shown in this Indian picture of the birth of the Mogul emperor Akbar's first son in 1569.

WHEN IT HAPPENED

1500 The game of real tennis becomes very popular in France.

1535 Angela Merici founds a teaching order of nuns called the Ursulines. Joining a convent is still one of the very few options apart from marriage open to women at this time.

1540 In Germany there is a fashion for men to wear jackets with huge padded shoulders and bright coloured doublets.

1590 In France women start to wear a whalebone farthingale under their dresses. It is shaped like a wheel and makes the skirt stand out as much as 60 centimetres from the hips.

1521 Hernán Cortés captures Tenochtitlán, the Aztec capital. Germany: The Diet of Worms, condemns Martin Luther as a heretic and excommunicates him (cuts him off from the Roman Catholic Church). England: Henry VIII is made 'Defender of the Faith' by Pope Leo X for opposing Luther. The Ottoman Turks capture Belgrade. Ferdinand Magellan dies in the Philippines.

1522 Italy: Emperor Charles V drives the French out of Milan. Spain: One ship from Magellan's expedition completes the first circumnavigation of the world. The Ottoman Turks take the island of Rhodes from the Knights of St John.

A sipahi or cavalryman of the Ottoman empire. In return for providing military service in times of war they received a land grant from the state. They remained important until the 18th century.

1523 Papal States: Clement VII is elected as pope. Sweden: Gustavus Vasa of Sweden leads the revolt against the Danish rulers of his country and is elected King Gustavus I of Sweden.

1524 Italy: France invades and recaptures Milan. England: The first turkey from South America is eaten at court.

1525 South America: Huayna Capac dies and civil war breaks out in the Inca empire, between Huascar, the 12th Sapa Inca, who rules in the south, and his brother, Atahualpa, who rules in the north. Italy: At the battle of Pavia, Francis I of France is captured by the Spaniards. He is released a year later in return for giving up his claim to Milan, Genoa and Naples. He fails to keep this promise and instead forms an alliance with Pope Clement VII, Milan, Venice and Florence against Charles V.

The Ottoman Empire

When Constantinople fell in 1453 (*see* pages 302–303), the Ottoman empire started its golden age. The former Christian capital of the Byzantine empire was renamed Istanbul and it became the centre of an empire which eventually covered more than 2.5 million square kilometres. At its peak, the Ottoman empire stretched from Algeria to Arabia and from Hungary to Egypt. Most of these conquests were made during the rule of Suleiman I who became sultan in 1520.

To his own people he was known as *Qanuni*, the Lawgiver, because he reformed administration and the legal system. However, Europeans called him Suleiman the Magnificent because of the splendour of his court and his military victories in Europe. These included a series of campaigns in which he captured Belgrade in Yugoslavia, the island of

▲ *Suleiman's greatest victory was at the battle of Mohacs in 1526 when he crushed the Hungarian army. This picture is taken from a painting commemorating the battle in which the king of Bohemia was also killed.*

Rhodes and the whole of Hungary. In 1529 his armies even reached Vienna, the capital of the Holy Roman Empire, but they failed to conquer it. The Turkish fleet, under the pirate Barbarossa (Khayr ad-Din Pasha), attacked and ravaged the coast of the Mediterranean.

Suleiman also waged three campaigns to the east against the Safavid empire of Persia (*see* pages 346–347). In these he gained control of Mesopotamia (Iraq), but the eastern border of the empire was never secure. Wars between the two empires lasted throughout the 16th century and helped to stop the Ottoman Turks advancing further into Europe.

When Suleiman died his son Selim II became sultan. He led a life of leisure while his ministers and generals ran the empire. By 1600 the Ottoman empire was in decline.

▲ *The women of the Ottoman empire led a secluded life. When they went outside the house, they had to be fully veiled and accompanied by a servant. They could only meet men from their own families.*

▼ *By 1566 the Ottoman empire stretched into three continents. Suleiman had built up a strong navy and won control of the Mediterranean. He also dominated the Red Sea and Persian Gulf.*

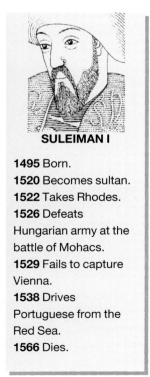

SULEIMAN I

1495 Born.
1520 Becomes sultan.
1522 Takes Rhodes.
1526 Defeats Hungarian army at the battle of Mohacs.
1529 Fails to capture Vienna.
1538 Drives Portuguese from the Red Sea.
1566 Dies.

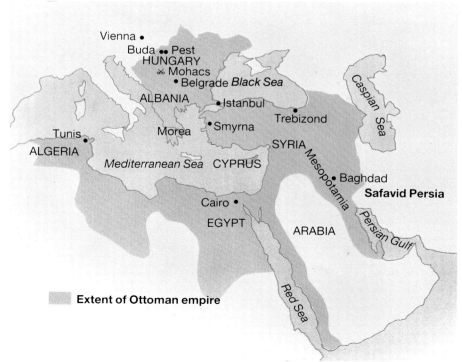

Vienna •
Buda •• Pest
HUNGARY
⚔ Mohacs
• Belgrade *Black Sea*
ALBANIA
• Istanbul
Morea • Smyrna Trebizond
Tunis •   *Caspian Sea*
ALGERIA
SYRIA
Mediterranean Sea CYPRUS   Mesopotamia
• Baghdad
Safavid Persia
Cairo •
EGYPT   ARABIA   *Persian Gulf*
Red Sea

▨ **Extent of Ottoman empire**

The Mogul Empire

Babur founded the Mogul empire when he invaded northern India from Afghanistan in 1526. He was a descendant of Tamerlane (*see* pages 272–273), who in turn claimed descent from Genghis Khan. The name Mogul is a variation of the word Mongol.

Babur and his followers were Muslims. When they invaded India, the Ottoman empire supplied them with guns and soldiers. Babur's troops also rode swift horses which easily outmanoeuvred the Indians' slower elephants. This helped them to defeat a much larger Indian army at a battle in which the sultan of Delhi was killed. After this victory, Babur made Delhi his capital.

When Babur died in 1530, his son Humayun became the next ruler. He could not hold the throne, however, and in 1540 he was chased out of India and into Persia. He returned in 1555 to win

▲ *The founders of the Mogul dynasty were* (from left to right): *Babur, Timur and Humayun. Here they are shown with their chief attendants.*

▼ *Babur only ruled over north India. Akbar expanded the empire to include lands to the east and south.*

BABUR

1483 Born in Ferghana, Central Asia of mixed Mongol and Turkish blood.
1495 Becomes ruler of Ferghana.
1526 Defeats the sultan of Dehli at the battle of Panipat, and becomes first Mogul emperor of India.
1530 Dies at Agra.

AKBAR

1542 Born.
1555 Becomes the third Mogul emperor.
1556–1562 Wins lands including the Punjab and Kabul.
1562 Marries a Rajput (Hindu) princess.
1563–1605 Wins Bengal, Kashmir and part of the Deccan.
1605 Dies.

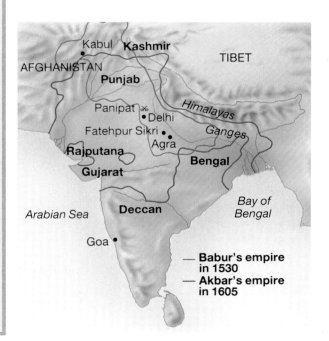

— Babur's empire in 1530
— Akbar's empire in 1605

the empire back, but before he could do so, he was killed in an accident. His 14-year-old son, Akbar, became emperor and ruled until his death in 1605.

Under Akbar, the Mogul empire expanded and flourished. He was a great military leader who defeated the neighbouring Rajputs and conquered Gujarat and Bengal. This was the richest province in the north of India. It produced rice and silk which provided Akbar with his main source of income.

Akbar was also a very wise ruler. Although he was a Muslim, many of his subjects were Hindu. To keep the peace he married a Hindu princess. He allowed his subjects freedom of worship and let them be tried according to their own religious laws. Akbar built schools for the children and also constructed a new capital city at Fatehpur Sikri. It combined Muslim and Hindu styles of architecture.

▼ *Although some people rebelled against Akbar, they were soon defeated. This picture shows the rebel Bahadur Khan submitting to him.*

1526 Central Europe: At the battle of Mohacs, the Ottoman Turks defeat and kill Louis II of Bohemia and Hungary. Ferdinand of Austria, brother of Charles V, succeeds to the Bohemian throne. A dispute over the Hungarian succession starts between Ferdinand and the Ottoman empire (to 1528). India: Babur defeats the last sultan of Delhi at Panipat and founds the Mogul empire.

1527 Papal States: Spanish and German troops sack Rome and capture the pope.

1528 Hungary: Ferdinand of Austria succeeds to the Hungarian throne. Switzerland: The first manual of surgery is written by Paracelsus, a physician.

An illustration from Babur's magnificent account of Hindustan, in northern India.

1529 England: Henry VIII dismisses Lord Chancellor Thomas Wolsey for failing to obtain the pope's consent to his divorce from Catherine of Aragon. Sir Thomas More is appointed Lord Chancellor. Henry VIII summons the 'Reformation Parliament' and sets about cutting ties with Rome. Europe: In the Peace of Cambrai between France and Spain, France renounces claims to Italy. The Treaty of Barcelona is signed by Pope Clement VII and Charles V. Austria: The Turks unsuccessfully besiege Vienna.

1530 Malta: Knights of St John are given the island by Charles V. England: Thomas Wolsey dies on his way to be tried for treason. Switzerland: Civil war breaks out between the Catholic and Protestant cantons. The Protestants are defeated.

The Conquistadores

Soon after the navigators had found their way to the Americas, Spanish adventurers, known as the *conquistadores* (conquerors), started to make their way to what they called the New World. After conquering many Caribbean islands, they started exploring the mainland of Central and South America in the hope of finding treasure.

In 1519 a group of about 500 Spanish soldiers, led by Hernán Cortés, attacked the Aztecs in their capital city of Tenochtitlán. The Aztec emperor, Montezuma, had been awaiting the return of the god-king Quetzalcóatl and thought that Cortés was he. Montezuma. allowed himself to be captured and Cortés ruled in his place. When Cortés went back to the coast, however, the Aztecs rebelled and defeated the Spaniards that were left behind. With the help of an interpreter, Cortés then won the support of neighbouring tribes who had been conquered by the Aztecs.

▲ Both Cortés and Pizarro lived in the West Indies before exploring the mainland of Central and South America. Cortés found the Aztec empire easily, but Pizarro had problems finding the Incas. He set out in 1530, but it took him three expeditions to find them.

▶ When Cortés and his men arrived in Tenochtitlán, they had with them horses and guns, both of which the Aztecs had never seen before. They also took a local interpreter called Dona Martina. She told them that the emperor Montezuma thought they were all gods because of their clothes. Because he believed this, Montezuma showered them with gifts. He also did not object when Cortés made him a prisoner and ruled the Aztecs in his place. He was deposed in 1521.

In 1521 he returned to Tenochtitlán and destroyed the city.

Another conquistador, Francisco Pizarro, landed in Peru in 1532 intending to conquer the Inca empire. A civil war was in progress there, between Huascar and Atahualpa who were the sons of Huayna Capac (*see* pages 326–327). Atahualpa killed Huascar, but Pizarro then had Atahualpa executed. The Incas soon surrendered and by 1533 their empire was in Spanish hands.

▲ *Atahualpa, the Inca ruler, tried to buy his freedom by filling a room with gold treasures and offering them to Pizarro, but Pizarro had him executed.*

CORTES

Hernán Cortés (1485–1547) was born into a noble Spanish family and lived in the West Indies as a young man. After conquering the Aztecs he returned to Spain and died there in poverty.

PIZARRO

Francisco Pizarro (c. 1475–1541) arrived in Panama in 1513. Hearing about the Incas, he marched on them in 1532. He founded Lima before being murdered by a rival in 1541.

1532 South America: Huascar is defeated and Francisco Pizarro begins his conquest of the Inca empire for Spain; he takes Atahualpa captive. England: Sir Thomas More resigns over the question of Henry VIII's divorce; Thomas Cranmer becomes archbishop of Canterbury. Germany: The Peace of Nuremberg allows some Protestants to practise their religion freely. France: Calvin starts the Protestant movement. Hungary: The Ottoman Turks invade but are defeated.

1533 South America: Francisco Pizarro captures the Inca captial, Cuzco, and conquers Peru. Atahualpa is executed for crimes against Spain. England: Henry VIII marries Anne Boleyn and is excommunicated by the pope. Eastern Europe: Peace is made between the Ottoman empire and Ferdinand of Austria. Russia: Ivan IV, also known as Ivan the Terrible, becomes ruler of Russia (to 1584), at the age of three.

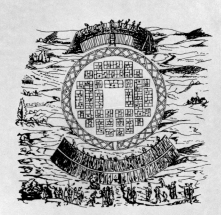

A map of Hochelaga, now Montreal, a Huron Indian town that was discovered by Jacques Cartier on his second voyage to America.

1534 England: By the Act of Supremacy, Henry VIII is declared supreme head of the Church in England. Spain: Ignatius Loyola founds the Society of Jesus, also known as Jesuits. Papal States: Paul III is elected as pope. Ottoman empire: The Ottoman Turks capture Tunis, Baghdad and Mesopotamia (Iraq).

Religion

This period saw splits in both the Islamic and the Christian worlds. The Islamic world was divided between the Sunnis, who thought that the leader of Islam should be chosen by the people, and the Shiites who thought that he should be descended from Muhammed.

Following the Reformation, the Christian world divided into Roman Catholics whose leader was the pope, and Protestants who were divided into many different groups. Catholic missionaries converted the Aztecs and Incas, but had less success in Japan and none at all in China. In India, Akbar's fair and wise government kept the peace between Muslims and Hindus.

◀ Many Native North Americans had no contact with Europeans at this time, so they followed their own religions without any interference. Their beliefs were closely tied to nature and magic. The most important religious person was the medicine man. He used plants and herbs to prepare cures and took part in religious and magic ceremonies.

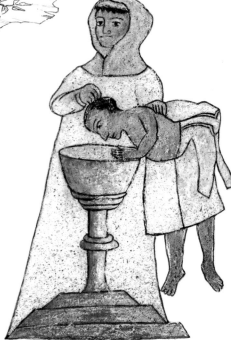

▶ In Central and South America, the Spanish conquistadores were soon followed by Roman Catholic missionaries. They were determined to win souls for God and convert the people there to Christianity. They did not hesitate to use force if other methods failed. They destroyed the Aztec and Inca temples and made the Native Americans build Christian churches in their place. Indians who refused to abandon their old gods were usually burned to death.

◀ During this period many new churches were built in Europe and old ones were extended or replaced. Those belonging to the Roman Catholic faith were usually very ornate, like this one at Pavia in Italy. It was started in 1491 and the outside was decorated using different coloured marbles. Roman Catholic churches had rich carvings, paintings and stained glass windows. In contrast, the new Protestant churches were very plain and simple in style.

► *Aztec priests used stone-bladed knives like this one to cut out the hearts of their victims. Every night 100 people were sacrificed to the god of war Huitzilopochtli.*

◄ *This cartoon is thought to be an anti-Lutheran picture. It is supposed to show that the devil dictated Luther's sermons to him.*

▼ *People found guilty of heresy (holding beliefs contrary to that of the established Church) could be burnt at the stake in punishment.*

WHEN IT HAPPENED

1517 The Reformation starts in Europe.
1519 In India Guru Nanak founds Sikhism.
1534 Ignatius Loyola founds the Society of Jesus, or Jesuits.
1536 Dissolution of the Monasteries in England.
1545 Meeting of the first Council of Trent to try and reform the Roman Catholic Church.
1549 St Francis Xavier arrives in Japan to convert the people to Christianity.
1560 The first Puritans preach in England.
1562 The French Wars of Religion start.

◄ *In the 16th century, Buddhism flourished in China and Japan, with many temples and thousands of monks. Around their temples in Japan, the Zen Buddhists laid out gardens of contemplation, like this one at Ryoan-ji in Kyoto, then the capital of Japan. It has no plants. Instead it has an oblong of raked white sand, with 15 rocks of different sizes set in it.*

1535 The French explorer Jacques Cartier navigates the St Lawrence River and claims Canada for France. Silver mining in Peru and Mexico greatly benefits Spain (the crown is entitled to one-fifth of any silver mined). The Spanish explore Chile. England: Sir Thomas More is executed for refusing to take the oath agreeing to the Act of Supremacy. Italy: Milan comes under Spanish control. War between France and Spain (to 1538).

1536 England: Anne Boleyn is executed and Henry VIII marries Jane Seymour. The Dissolution of the Monasteries starts (completed 1540). The money from selling monastic lands is used to help pay for wars with France. The Pilgrimage of Grace, a Catholic uprising in the north, is suppressed. The German artist Hans Holbein becomes court painter to Henry VIII. Switzerland: Calvin leads the Protestants in Geneva. Italy: France invades Savoy and Piedmont and makes an alliance with the Ottoman Turks.

1537 England: Jane Seymour dies after the birth of a son, the future Edward VI.

1539 Holy Roman Empire: The Truce of Frankfurt is made between Charles V and the Protestant princes of the empire.

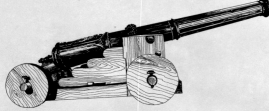

This bronze gun was found in the wreck of the Mary Rose *which sank in 1544.*

1540 England: Henry VIII marries Anne of Cleves following negotiations by Thomas Cromwell. Henry soon divorces her and marries Catherine Howard. Thomas Cromwell is executed for treason. Low Countries: Gerhardus Mercator finishes his first map of the world. Italy: Philip, son of Charles V, is made duke of Milan. Papal States: Pope Paul III approves Ignatius Loyola's Society of Jesus.

The Spanish Empire

After the conquest of the Aztecs and the Incas, the king of Spain added their territories to his empire. He divided the lands into two viceroyalties, each ruled by a viceroy. The Aztec empire became the Viceroyalty of New Spain in 1535. Later in the 16th century it also included parts of California, Arizona and New Mexico. The land of the Incas became the Viceroyalty of Peru.

Many people from Spain went to live in the new Spanish empire. The colonies were ruled by the Council of the Indies based in Spain. Many of the laws made for the colonies show that the Spanish government tried to make sure that the

---

NEW FOODS FOR EUROPE

The Spanish explorers brought many new foods back to Europe. These included pineapples, tomatoes, capsicums and sunflowers which were grown for their seeds. They found the potato in the high mountains of Peru and took some samples back to Europe where at first they were grown for their flowers, rather than for food. The Aztecs used cocoa beans as money and also ground them to make a chocolate drink. In 1528 Cortés took some beans to Spain and cocoa gradually became a popular drink in Europe. The Spanish and the Portuguese introduced sugar cane to the West Indies and Brazil. Native American slaves first worked on the plantations then African slaves were brought over.

▲ The Spanish exploited the gold and silver of the New World. The harsh conditions and new diseases brought by the Spanish meant the population of Mexico fell from 25 million in 1519 to just over 1 million in 1600.

▼ Spain tried to stop other countries trading with its empire, but did not succeed. By 1600 France, England and the Netherlands were challenging its might.

Native Americans were not ill-treated. But it was impossible to prevent the ruling Spaniards from treating them very very cruelly. The Native Americans were forced to mine silver and to work as slaves. Thousands died because they had no resistance to European diseases such as measles and smallpox.

The conquistadores and colonists were followed by Spanish missionaries. They destroyed the existing temples and idols and set up Roman Catholic churches in their place. They tried to force all the Indians to become Christians.

The Spanish empire continued to expand during the reign of Philip II (1556–1598). Most of the islands of the Philippines were conquered in 1571. Then King Sebastian of Portugal was killed in battle against the Moroccans in north Africa in 1578. As Philip was Sebastian's nearest relative, he was able to add the Portuguese empire to his own.

By 1600 the Spanish empire was the biggest in the world, but it had begun to lose its power. Philip's desire to stamp out heresy had led him into wars which used up most of the gold and silver that had been taken from the New World.

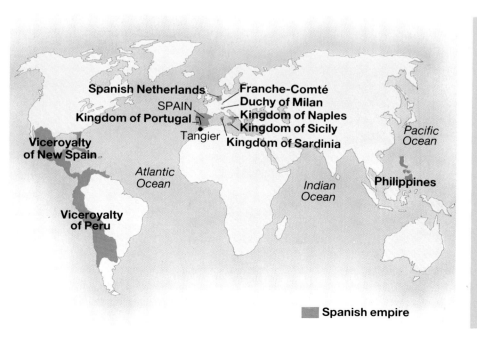

Spanish Netherlands
Franche-Comté
SPAIN
Duchy of Milan
Kingdom of Portugal
Kingdom of Naples
Tangier
Kingdom of Sicily
Kingdom of Sardinia
Viceroyalty of New Spain
Pacific Ocean
Atlantic Ocean
Indian Ocean
Philippines
Viceroyalty of Peru

■ Spanish empire

EL DORADO

The conquistadores were spurred on in their explorations by the legend of *El Dorado* which means 'the Golden Man', whose kingdom was said to be full of gold. This promised land was never found and silver gradually became more important. It eventually made up 90 per cent of the precious metals sent back to Spain.

1541 North America: Hernondo de Soto discovers the Mississippi. Scotland: John Knox brings the Reformation to Scotland. Ottoman empire: The Ottoman Turks conquer Hungary.

1542 England: Catherine Howard is executed. Scotland: At the battle of Solway Moss, James V of Scotland is killed. His one-week-old daughter, Mary, becomes queen of Scots (to 1567), with her French mother, Mary of Guise, as her regent. Japan: The first Portuguese sailors arrive.

1543 England: Henry VIII marries Catherine Parr and forms an alliance with Charles V. Europe: Vesalius publishes his work on human anatomy. Poland: On his deathbed, the astronomer and priest Nicolas Copernicus states that the Earth moves around the Sun.

A silver pomander made in about 1580. It carried perfume to keep away disease.

1544 France: Henry VIII and Charles V invade France. Western Europe: Spain and France sign The Treaty of Crepy.

1545 Europe: Pope Paul III opens the Council of Trent which, under Jesuit guidance, is to reform the Roman Catholic Church.

1547 England: Henry VIII dies and his 10-year-old son becomes King Edward VI of England (to 1553). The Duke of Somerset acts as Lord Protector. France: Francis I dies and his son Henry II succeeds to the throne (to 1559). Germany: Charles V defeats the Protestant Schmalkaldic League at the battle of Muhlberg. Russia: Ivan IV is crowned tsar, or emperor, of Russia. France: French becomes the official language, rather than Latin.

The Counter-Reformation

In 1522 Pope Adrian VI admitted there were many problems in the Roman Catholic Church, but he died before he could start putting them right. Nothing more was done until 1534, when Paul III became pope. He started to reform the Church in a movement known as the Counter-Reformation. He began by encouraging the preaching and missionary work of an Italian order of friars, called the Capuchins. Six years later he approved the founding of the Society of Jesus, or Jesuits, which had been founded by Ignatius Loyola to spread Catholicism.

With the encouragement of the Holy Roman Emperor, Pope Paul III called a meeting known as the Council of Trent in 1545 to decide what else needed to be done to reform the Roman Catholic Church. One of the suggestions was better education for clergymen and Church colleges, called seminaries, were set up. The Council of Trent also decided that monks, nuns and priests should obey their vows of poverty.

▲ *The religious conflict in this period led to an inceased concern with witchcraft. Both Catholics and Protestants began witch hunts which often led to harmless women being burned or drowned.*

LOYOLA

Ignatius Loyola (1491–1556) was born in Spain. He turned to religion after being wounded in battle. In 1534 he founded the Society of Jesus. This aimed to spread the Catholic faith largely through teaching and set up missions as far away as India, China, and South America.

ERASMUS

Desiderius Erasmus (c. 1467–1536), born in the Netherlands, was a traveller and scholar. He published an edition of the Greek New Testament. He was a Catholic, but his views clashed with those of the Church. In 1559 his books were placed on the Index of forbidden books.

▲ The Council of Trent met three times between 1545 and 1563. It reformed the Roman Catholic Church and tried to stop the spread of Protestantism.

In 1554 Charles V's son, Philip, the future king Phillip II of Spain, married Mary I of England, daughter of Henry VIII and Catherine of Aragon. Mary had made England Catholic again when she came to the throne in 1553. The marriage was a failure and when Mary died England became Protestant again. Later Philip tried to restore Catholicism in England and the Netherlands by force. He failed and in the process also helped to ruin Spain's economy.

▼ The Spanish Inquisition questioned people accused of heresy. This included reading books that were forbidden by the Catholic church, and having Protestant beliefs. Heretics were burned at the stake.

The Habsburgs

The Habsburg family dominated European politics for over 600 years from the 13th century onward. It took its name from the family castle in Switzerland which was called Habichtsburg or 'Hawk's Castle'. By the 13th century Austria and Styria formed part of their lands and, from 1438 onwards, the Holy Roman emperor was nearly always a member of the Habsburg family. In the late 15th century, Maximilian I made sure that their power would continue by arranging very advantageous marriages for his family. His son, Philip of Burgundy, was married to Joanna the Mad, a daughter of Ferdinand and Isabella of Spain. Their son, who became Charles V, was the most powerful Habsburg of all.

When Philip died in 1506, Charles inherited Burgundy and the Netherlands. In 1516 Ferdinand of Spain left him Spain and Naples, and in

▼ After Charles died, Austrian Habsburgs ruled the Holy Roman Empire and Spanish Habsburgs ruled Spain, the Netherlands and part of Italy.

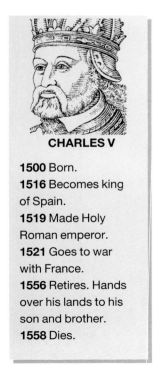

CHARLES V

1500 Born.
1516 Becomes king of Spain.
1519 Made Holy Roman emperor.
1521 Goes to war with France.
1556 Retires. Hands over his lands to his son and brother.
1558 Dies.

— Extent of Holy Roman Empire

Habsburg lands

DENMARK

NETHERLANDS

FRANCE

GERMANY

SWITZERLAND AUSTRIA

HUNGARY

Burgundy

Navarre

PORTUGAL

SPAIN Aragon

Castile

FLORENCE PAPAL STATES

Ottoman empire

NAPLES

Kingdom of Sardinia

TUNIS SICILY

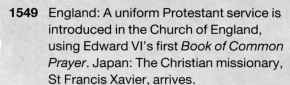

◄ *Rudolf IV founded Habsburg power. He was elected king of Germany and became Holy Roman emperor although he was never crowned. The Holy Roman Empire remained in Habsburg hands until 1806.*

1519 he inherited the Holy Roman Empire from Maximilian. This led to rivalry with Francis I of France, who also wanted to be Holy Roman emperor, and their countries were at war for most of Charles's reign.

A devout Catholic, Charles also had to deal with problems in the Holy Roman Empire caused by people in Germany who had become Protestants after the Reformation (*see* pages 354–355). In 1546 Charles took up arms against some of them who had formed the League of Schmalkalden. He defeated them in 1547, but four years later he was forced to agree to their demands.

By 1556, Charles was exhausted by all these wars. He retired to a monastery, having divided his lands between his son, Philip (who ruled Spain and the Netherlands) and his brother, Ferdinand (who ruled Germany and Austria).

THE HOLY ROMAN EMPIRE

First used in the 13th century, the double-headed eagle was the emblem of the Holy Roman Empire. The eagle was a symbol of power, but in the 16th century the power of the emperors began to decline. Some of the German states grew more powerful and wanted to become independent of the Holy Roman Empire. This was especially true

after the Reformation when many states in northern Germany became Protestant while the Holy Roman emperor remained Roman Catholic. In the 17th century this led to the Thirty Years War (*see* pages 416–417).

1549 England: A uniform Protestant service is introduced in the Church of England, using Edward VI's first *Book of Common Prayer*. Japan: The Christian missionary, St Francis Xavier, arrives.

1550 Papal States: Julius III becomes pope (to 1555). England: The Duke of Northumberland replaces the Duke of Somerset as Protector of Edward VI.

Violins as we know them today appeared in about the middle of the 16th century.

1551 War starts between the Ottoman Turks and Hungary (to 1562).

1552 War breaks out between Spain and France (to 1556). France seizes Toul, Metz and Verdun. England: Second *Book of Common Prayer*.

1553 England: On death of Edward VI, Lady Jane Grey is proclaimed queen of England by the Duke of Northumberland. Her reign lasts nine days. Mary I, daughter of Henry VIII and Catherine of Aragon, then becomes queen (to 1558). She is a devout Roman Catholic.

1554 England: Lady Jane Grey is executed. Mary I marries Philip, heir to throne of Spain, on condition that he will not be allowed to rule England in the event of her death. North Africa: The Ottoman Turks start to conquer the coast.

1555 England: With Mary on the throne England returns to Roman Catholicism. Protestants are persecuted and about 300, including Thomas Cranmer, are burned at the stake. Papal States: Paul IV is elected pope. Germany: At the Peace of Augsburg, Protestant princes are granted freedom of worship and the right to introduce the Reformation into their own territories. Russia: Building starts on St Basil's Cathedral in Moscow. India: Akbar, grandson of Babur, becomes Mogul emperor (to 1605).

Science and Technology

The revival of learning in 15th century Europe led people to start observing the world about them and do experiments, rather than just accept what they were told. Sometimes this led to clashes with the Church, when new ideas were contrary to the Church's teachings. Even though scientists were threatened with stern punishments, many brilliant ideas and inventions were produced such as the first successful watch, invented in 1504, and the microscope, invented in the 1590. People also studied the human body and in 1543 Andreas Vesalius published some of the first accurate descriptions of human anatomy. His teachings, however, were unpopular.

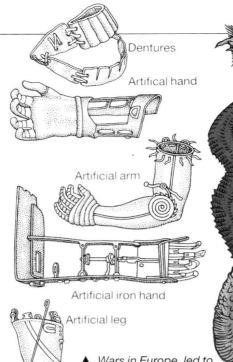

Dentures

Artifical hand

Artificial arm

Artificial iron hand

Artificial leg

▲ Wars in Europe, led to growing interest in surgery. Amboise Pare, a great French surgeon, designed useful aids for crippled soldiers. His artificial hand had fingers which moved by springs and cog-wheels.

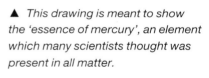

▲ This drawing is meant to show the 'essence of mercury', an element which many scientists thought was present in all matter.

▼ During the Renaissance people began to study mathematics seriously. This helped them with their scientific experiments.

▼ Leonardo da Vinci drew many sketches of flying-machines. In this one a man flaps the four wings with a system of pulleys and treadles.

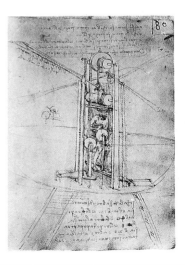

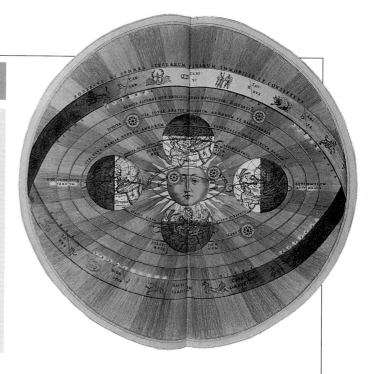

WHEN IT HAPPENED

1504 In Germany Peter Heinlein invents a watch.

1543 Nicolas Copernicus publishes his theory that the Earth moves round the Sun.

1556 *De Re Metallica*, one of the first books on mining and mineralogy, is published in Germany. Although it is a scientific work, the author warns of underground demons.

1598 Tycho Brahe moves from Denmark to Prague where Kepler becomes his student. After Brahe's death, Kepler's studies force him to agree with Copernicus' findings.

1600 Giordano Bruno is burnt at the stake by the Spanish Inquisition for saying that the Earth moves round the Sun.

▶ *In the 16th century scientists had many strange theories to explain reproduction. This drawing shows a lamb growing like a plant. They also believed that more minerals would grow underground to replace those removed by mining.*

▲ *This is the Solar System as described by Nicolas Copernicus in 1543. He said that the Earth and planets moved round the Sun and that the Earth turned on its own axis every day. Many people thought that this was not only against the teachings of the Church, but against common sense. They thought that if the Earth turned it would make a great wind.*

◀ *Tycho Brahe (1546–1601) was a Danish astronomer who came to the attention of King Frederick II of Denmark after observing a star called a nova. The king had two observatories built for him on the island of Hveen. In the observatory shown here he had a library, laboratory, living apartments and rooms for his instruments. From his observations he believed that the planets moved round the Sun, but that the Sun then moved round the Earth. The telescope had not been invented then, but Brahe established the positions of 777 stars by naked-eye observations.*

Elizabethan England

During the reign of Queen Elizabeth I, England became a prosperous trading nation. From the start of the 16th century, sailors from Devon and Cornwall sailed across the Atlantic to fish for cod in the seas off Newfoundland. Then English sailors started trading with Spanish America. In 1562 the seaman John Hawkins bought slaves in Sierra Leone, Africa, and took them to Hispaniola in the West Indies where he traded them for hides and sugar. He sold these goods in England for such a profit that Queen Elizabeth herself invested money in his next voyage.

Other sailors turned to piracy, attacking Spanish treasure ships taking silver back from America. This, and the fact that Elizabeth had sent a military force to the Netherlands to help Dutch

DRAKE

Francis Drake (c. 1543 –1596) was born in Devon. He became a sea captain and later an admiral. His first voyages were to Guinea and the West Indies. In 1580 he became the first Englishman to sail round the world in his ship the *Golden Hind*. He helped defeat the Spanish Armada.

ELIZABETH I

1533 Born. Only child of Henry VIII and Anne Boleyn.
1558 Becomes queen of England and Ireland on her sister Mary's death.
1559–1563 Sets up a moderate Protestant Church in England.
1588 English fleet defeats the Spanish Armada.
1603 Dies.

▶ *When this portrait was painted after England's victory over the Spanish Armada, Elizabeth was 56 years old. Well-educated and a skilful politician, she was made to look younger as a symbol of her power. She never married and was succeeded by James VI.*

◀ *Philip II sent his Invincible Armada to attack England in August 1588. The Spanish had more ships, but the English sailors knew the seas better. The English ships were more manoeuvrable than the heavy Spanish galleons and defeated the Armada off Gravelines in France.*

SHAKESPEARE

One of the most famous Elizabethans was the playwright and poet William Shakespeare. He was born in the market town of Stratford-on-Avon in 1564, the son of a rich tradesman. He married Anne Hathaway in 1582 and they had three children. After becoming an actor in London, he wrote his first four plays between 1589 and 1592. These were *Richard III* and the three parts of *Henry VI*. Between 1593 and 1600 he wrote comedies, including *A Midsummer Night's Dream* and *The Taming of the Shrew*. By 1599 he held shares in the Globe Theatre at Southwark in London. He then started to write tragedies, including *Hamlet* and *Macbeth*. Shakespeare lived until 1616 and wrote 37 plays in all.

rebels in their fight against Spanish rule (*see* pages 386–387), angered Philip II of Spain so much that in 1588 he sent a fleet of fighting ships called the Armada to attack England. It was unsuccessful but the war with Spain continued until after Elizabeth's death in 1603.

England prospered in spite of war with Spain. Elizabeth was a hard-working and

1556 Holy Roman Empire: Charles V abdicates. Spain and its colonies, the Netherlands, Naples, Milan and Franche-Comté are to go to his son Philip. The Holy Roman Empire and the Habsburg lands go to Charles' brother, Ferdinand. An alliance is made between Pope Paul IV and Henry II of France. India: By his victory at the battle of Panipat, Babur's grandson, Akbar, establishes his rule as Mogul emperor.

Elizabethan women wore elaborate clothes such as this jewelled stomacher, worn over the chest and stomach.

1557 At the battle of St Quentin, Spain and England defeat France. The Livonian War, a dispute over the succession to territories in the Balkans, between Poland, Russia, Sweden and Denmark, starts (to 1582). Russia invades Poland. China: Portuguese traders are allowed to settle in Macao.

1558 France: England loses Calais, its last possession in France. England: Mary dies and is succeeded by Elizabeth I (to 1603). Catholic legislation in England is repealed. Mary, Queen of Scots, marries Francis, Dauphin (heir to the throne) of France. Holy Roman Empire: Ferdinand I becomes emperor (to 1564). Papal States: Pius IV becomes pope (to 1565).

1559 The Treaty of Cateau-Cambresis ends war between Spain and France; France gives up all its conquests except Toul, Metz and Verdun. Spain controls most of Italy. The king of France, Henry II, dies of a head wound received in a tournament celebrating the peace. His son, Francis II becomes king (to 1560) at the age of 16.

1560 Scotland: The Treaty of Berwick is made between Elizabeth I and Scottish reformers and the Church of Scotland is founded. The Treaty of Edinburgh is agreed between England, Scotland and France. England: The first Puritans appear. Many of them are Protestants who went abroad to escape persecution in the reign of Mary I. They want to purify the Church of England of anything left over from Roman Catholicism. France: Francis II dies and is succeeded by his 10-year-old brother, Charles IX (to 1574). Catherine de Medici, widow of Henry II, rules France as regent. The Huguenots, (French Protestants) try to overthrow the Guise family who are strong supporters of the Catholic cause. Jean Nicot imports tobacco seeds and leaves into France (nicotine is named after him).

A contemporary illustration of the beheading of Mary, Queen of Scots in 1587. Elizabeth I had kept her under guard for 18 years before signing her death warrant.

1561 Scotland: Mary, Queen of Scots and widow of Francis II, returns to Scotland. Spain: Madrid becomes the capital. England: The English sea captain, John Hawkins, starts England's involvement in the slave trade when he takes 300 African slaves from a Portuguese ship bound for Brazil. India: Portuguese monks in Goa introduce printing to India.

▲ *Elizabeth I travelled a great deal around England so that people could see her. She took her courtiers with her and stayed at large country houses. After hunting, she often enjoyed an elaborate meal in the open air.*

intelligent monarch. She established a rule with the aid of her chief adviser, William Cecil, that made her popular with her people. Art, music and literature flourished as the country enjoyed a time of stability.

Elizabeth hoped to satisfy most of her subjects by re-establishing the Church of England along mostly Protestant lines. She passed two laws called the Religious Settlement of 1559. Although Catholics and Protestants alike criticized her settlement for being too moderate, there was no open warfare and Protestantism was slowly re-established.

Under Elizabeth's rule the textile and iron industries expanded and towns grew in size. Poor Laws were passed recognizing that some people might be genuinely unable to find employment and were in need of support from the Parish. The Poor Laws were also designed to try to prevent starvation in years when the harvest failed.

Mary, Queen of Scots

Mary became queen of Scotland in 1542 when she was just one week old. Her father, James V, was the nephew of Henry VIII and this eventually led Mary to claim the English throne. Mary's mother was Mary of Guise. She took Mary to France in 1547 and brought her up at the French court. In 1558 Mary married the *Dauphin* (heir to the French throne), soon to be Francis II. He died two years later and in 1561 Mary returned to Scotland.

By this time Scotland was a Protestant country, but Mary was a Catholic. She married Lord Darnley, her Catholic cousin, and they had a son, later James VI. When Mary tired of Darnley, she became friendly with her private secretary, David Rizzio. He was murdered in 1566 and later Darnley died when his house was blown up. The Earl of Bothwell was thought to be involved. When Mary married him, the Scottish lords rebelled and forced her to abdicate. In 1568 she fled to England where she was kept until her execution in 1587.

MARY

1542 Born.
1558 Marries the Dauphin Francis.
1560 Is widowed.
1561 Returns to Scotland.
1565 Marries Lord Henry Stuart Darnley.
1567 Marries the Earl of Bothwell. Loses battle of Carberry to Scottish lords and flees to England.
1587 Is executed.

KNOX

John Knox was a Scot who became attracted to Protestantism in 1543. He fled to Geneva in 1553 and met John Calvin. In 1558 he wrote *The First Blast of the Trumpet Against the Monstrous Regiment of Women*, protesting against Mary of Guise who ruled Scotland for her daughter.

▼ *After nearly twenty years of imprisonment, Mary was executed at Fotheringhay Castle in 1587 on a charge of treason. She was said to have plotted against Elizabeth I of England many times.*

French Wars of Religion

The spread of the Protestant faith led to problems in some parts of Europe. In France, the majority of the people stayed Roman Catholic, but the number of Protestants was growing. They were called Huguenots and at first they were tolerated.

King Henry II of France died in 1559 from an injury he received while celebrating the Peace of Cateau-Cambresis between France and Spain. His oldest son, Francis, succeeded him, but he died the following year.

Ten-year-old Charles then became king of France. He was under the complete control of his mother, Catherine de Medici. She supported the Catholics and objected when Charles came under the influence of the Huguenot leader, Admiral Gaspard de Coligny, in 1572.

▲ *Henry IV of France signed the Edict of Nantes in 1598. This brought the French Wars of Religion to an end because it gave the Huguenots freedom to worship as they wanted.*

▼ *The St Bartholomew's Day Massacre started in Paris on August 24 1572. As many as 20,000 Huguenots may have been killed throughout France in the course of that day and the next.*

CATHERINE DE MEDICI

Catherine de Medici (1519–1589) was born in Italy, the daughter of Lorenzo de Medici, Duke of Urbino. She married Henry II of France in 1533. She acted as regent for their second son, Charles IX, but her influence waned in Henry III's reign.

HENRY OF NAVARRE

1553 Born.
1572 Becomes king of Navarre and marries Margaret of Valois. Is held prisoner at court.
1589 Becomes Henry IV of France, the first Bourbon king.
1593 Converts to Catholicism.
1600 Marries Marie de Medici.
1610 Dies.

When an attempt to have Coligny assassinated failed, Catherine plotted a massacre of the leading Huguenots who were in Paris for the marriage of her daughter, Margaret, to the Huguenot Henry of Navarre. The killings began at dawn on St Bartholomew's Day and were repeated all over France. Coligny was killed, but Henry was spared.

In 1574 Henry III, another son of Catherine de Medici, became king of France. He was also influenced by his mother and the civil war continued. In 1585 he banned the Protestant religion, and the War of the Three Henrys started.

It involved Henry III of France, the Huguenot Henry of Navarre and the Catholic Henry of Guise. The war only ended in 1589 after Henry III had Henry of Guise murdered for trying to seize the throne. Henry III was then assassinated by a fanatical monk, and Henry of Navarre, his rightful heir, became King Henry IV of France.

1562 France: The Wars of Religion start in France, after the murder of over 60 Huguenots by the Guise family during a Protestant church service. Ireland: The Earl of Tyrone leads two unsuccessful rebellions against Queen Elizabeth I. The Ottoman Turks sign a eight-year truce with the Holy Roman Empire.

1563 England: The Thirty-Nine Articles combining Protestant beliefs with Roman Catholic organization and stating the ruling monarch is the head of the church, are adopted. English soldiers catch the plague while in France and bring it back to England; it kills over 20,000 people in London alone. Russia: Ivan the Terrible, conquers part of Livonia.

1564 Western Europe: The Peace of Troyes ends the war between England and France. Holy Roman Empire: Ferdinand I dies and is succeeded by his son, Maximilian II (to 1576). Europe: Michelangelo and John Calvin die. William Shakespeare and Galileo Galilei are born (Shakespeare dies 1616, Galileo 1642).

1565 Russia: A 'reign of terror' begins as Ivan the Terrible sets out to destroy the power of the nobles. America: Pedro Menendez de Aviles founds the first European colony in North America at St Augustine in Florida. Scotland: Mary, Queen of Scots, marries her cousin, Lord Darnley. Malta: The Ottoman Turks besiege Malta, but are defeated by the Knights of St John. Switzerland: First known use of pencils. England: Sir John Hawkins introduces sweet potatoes, and possibly tobacco as well.

During the reign of Henry IV, the French began breeding silk worms. This activity grew to become a national industry of France.

Society and Government

This period saw changes in both society and government in Europe. In many places the decline of the feudal system meant people were able to leave the land and look for work in towns if they wanted to. More powerful kings emerged, especially in England, France and Spain. They ruled over the whole of their countries and controlled the rich noblemen more successfully than their predecessors had.

Other parts of the world were governed differently. In the Inca empire, the old, the frail and the young were looked after by the state in a way which would not be equalled in Europe for over 400 years, but healthy young people were still sacrificed to the gods. In China, and later in Mogul India, the emperor's word was law, but both countries had a vast number of civil servants to make sure everyone obeyed. In the Ottoman empire women had to live in a special part of the house called a *harem* and were not allowed to meet any men from outside their immediate families.

▲ In North America, Great Plains Indians led a nomadic life hunting the buffalo. Different tribes had different customs, but story telling was an important part of all their cultures. Tribal customs and lore were passed from one generation to the next by word of mouth. A tribal council settled quarrels.

▼ Members of the Aztec royal family were carried round on litters. No one was allowed to look at the emperor and if they did they were risking death. Tribes conquered by the Aztecs had to send them tributes, while the army went to war to capture more people to sacrifice to the gods in Tenochtitlán.

▲ Utopia, *by the English lawyer and scholar, Sir Thomas More, was published in 1516. It was about a mythical island with an ideal social system; everyone shared equally in government, education and wars.*

WHEN IT HAPPENED

1498 Girolamo Savanorola is burned for heresy by his political rivals in Florence.

1513 Machiavelli writes *The Prince*. He says that all actions are fair to secure a stable state.

1520 Suleiman I becomes Ottoman emperor and reforms the laws and administration.

1555 In Russia Ivan IV reforms the legal code and local administration.

1572 Each parish in England is allowed to levy a rate from its parishoners to help the poor.

▶ *Leonardo Loredano was doge of the Venetian Republic from 1501 to 1521. Although he was head of state, the real power was in the hands of the Great Council whose members came from the leading families of Venice.*

▶ *To be pope was to be one of the most powerful men in the world. He not only ruled his own country, but, before the Reformation, was responsible for the spiritual welfare of nearly everyone in Europe (and later on of people all over the world). During the 15th and early 16th centuries, some popes worked hard to advance the fortunes of their own families. Pope Sixtus IV, shown here with four of his nephews, helped one of them to become Pope Julius II.*

Russia

Until the middle of the 15th century, much of southern Russia was under the control of the Mongol rulers of the Golden Horde (*see* pages 272–273) who were also known as Tartars. In 1462, however, a new ruler came to the throne of Muscovy, a small region of Russia that included Moscow. Ivan III, also known as 'the Great', succeeded in making his lands independent of the khanate of the Golden Horde. In 1472 he married the niece of the last Byzantine emperor and appointed himself as protector of the Eastern Orthodox Church.

By 1480 he had brought Novgorod and other cities under his control and called himself the ruler of all Russia. He made Moscow his capital and rebuilt its *kremlin* (citadel) which had been damaged by fire. When Ivan III died, he was succeeded by his son Vasili. Vasili ruled until 1533, then he was succeeded by Ivan IV, his three-year-old son.

IVAN III

1440 Born.
1462 Succeeds to the throne of Moscow.
1471–1478 Invades Novgorod three times before finally conquering it.
1480 Becomes ruler of all Russia.
1497 Introduces a new legal code.
1505 Dies an alcoholic.

IVAN IV

1530 Born.
1547 Is crowned tsar and grand prince of all Russia.
1547–1549 Pushes through legal and administrative reforms.
1565 Starts a 'reign of terror' to break the power of the nobility.
1581 Kills his heir, Ivan.
1584 Dies insane.

▼ *The Kremlin was the centre of Moscow. It was like a fort and many palaces, churches and cathedrals were built within the protection of its walls.*

▲ *St Basil's Cathedral in Moscow was constructed between 1555 and 1560 to celebrate Ivan IV's victories in Kazan and Astrakhan.*

Ivan IV also became known as Ivan the Terrible. He was the Grand Prince of Muscovy from 1533 to 1584 and was crowned as the first *tsar* (emperor) of Russia in 1547. His harsh upbringing left him with a violent and unpredictable character, but his nickname meant 'Awe-inspiring' rather than 'Terrible'.

He changed the legal system and local government as well as reforming trading links with England and other European countries. Ivan also expanded his lands by capturing Kazan and Astrakhan from the Tartars. From 1581 he started to bring Siberia under his control.

In that same year, he killed his eldest son in a fit of rage and so was succeeded by his second son, Fyodor. Boris Godunov acted as regent until Fyodor died in 1598, then he became tsar.

1566 Papal States: Cardinal Michaele Ghislieri is elected as Pope Pius V (to 1572). Netherlands: Religious riots break out between Catholics and the followers of John Calvin. Scotland: Mary, Queen of Scots gives birth to a son, the future James VI of Scotland. Ottoman empire: Suleiman the Magnificent dies and is succeeded by his son, Selim II (to 1574).

1567 In Brazil the Portuguese found Rio de Janeiro. Netherlands: The Duke of Alba is sent from Spain to quell the riots. Scotland: Lord Darnley, husband of Mary, Queen of Scots, is murdered, probably by the Earl of Bothwell who pretends to kidnap Mary; they are married in a Protestant ceremony. Later, Mary is forced to abdicate. Her son succeeds to the throne as James VI.

1568 An 80-year-long war of independence starts between the Netherlands and Spain. Mary, Queen of Scots escapes to England, but is held by Elizabeth I. Selim II of the Ottoman empire and Maximilian II of the Holy Roman Empire make a peace agreement which results in the Sultan receiving large annual payments from the emperor.

1569 Poland: The Union of Lublin merges Poland and Lithuania under Sigismund II of Poland. India: The Mogul emperor Akbar conquers Rajputana.

Grand Prince Ivan III married the niece of the last Byzantine emperor. He took the double-headed eagle of the Byzantine empire as his emblem.

1570 France: The Peace of St Germain-en-Laye ends the Third War of Religion, giving the Huguenots conditional freedom of worship. Ottoman empire: The Ottoman Turks attack Cyprus and declare war on Venice for refusing to hand over control of Cyprus. Russia: Ivan IV razes Novgorod.

1571  At the battle of Lepanto in the Mediterranean, a combined Papal and Venetian fleet under Don John of Austria defeats the Ottoman Turks under Ali Pasha. The Ottoman fleet loses all but 40 of its 230 galleys, while the Christian fleet lose just 12 ships. East Africa: Bornu empire in the Sudan reaches its greatest extent under Idris III.

1572 Papal States: Pope Pius V dies and is succeeded by Pope Gregory XIII (to 1585). France: Over 20,000 Huguenots are killed in the St Bartholomew's Day Massacre. England: Ben Jonson, dramatist, and John Donne, poet, are born (Jonson dies 1637, Donne 1631).

Iznik pottery of the Ottoman empire was influenced by Persian craftsmen. The pieces were often decorated with sailing vessels.

1573 Ottoman empire: Venice abandons Cyprus and makes peace with the Ottoman Turks. North Africa: Don John captures Tunis from the Ottoman Turks. India: The Mogul emperor Akbar conquers Gujurat. China: The Ming emperor Wan Li comes to power (to 1620). Italy: Michelangelo Caravaggio is born (dies 1610).

1574 France: Charles IX dies and his brother, Henry III, succeeds him (to 1589). North Africa: The Ottoman empire regains Tunis from Spain. Southern Africa: The Portuguese begin to settle in Angola.

1575 Spain faces bankruptcy and cannot afford to pay its troops in the Netherlands. Plague sweeps through Italy and Sicily.

Mediterranean Struggle

The Ottoman empire tried to gain control of the Mediterranean as its navy grew powerful during the reign of Suleiman the Magnificent (*see* pages 358–359). In 1522 it conquered the island of Rhodes where the Christian order of the Knights of St John (also called the Knights Hospitaller), had lived since 1282. This left the Knights without a home until the Holy Roman Emperor Charles V gave them the island of Malta in 1530. The Knights remained at war with the Muslim Turks over religion.

In May 1565 Suleiman decided to attack the Knights of St John and besieged Malta with a large fleet of ships. There were four times as many Turks as Knights, but the Knights had a strong leader in Jean Parisot de la Valette. Fighting continued until September

▼ *The leader of the Knights of St John, Jean Parisot de la Valette, founded a heavily fortified city to defend the island of Malta. It was called Valetta in his honour.*

▶ *At Lepanto, Don John of Austria commanded 204 galleys and 6 galleasses (huge oar-driven ships) against 230 Turkish galleys. The Turks lost all but 40 ships, and their hopes of controlling the Mediterranean.*

► *In the 16th century, the Ottoman empire and the Holy Roman Empire clashed on land and sea. The Ottoman Turks controlled the south and east of the Mediterranean, while the Holy Roman Empire, with Spain, controlled the west and Italy. Suleiman was followed by weaker rulers and the power of the Turks declined.*

when reinforcements arrived from Sicily, and the Turks withdrew.

Selim II then tried to expand the Ottoman empire by invading Cyprus in 1570. At that time Cyprus belonged to the Venetians. They immediately appealed to Pope Pius V for help and he assembled a fleet from the navies of Venice, Spain and the Papal States under the command of Don John of Austria. This fleet met the Turkish galleys at the battle of Lepanto off Greece in October 1571, and defeated them in three hours.

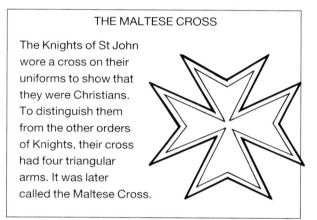

THE MALTESE CROSS

The Knights of St John wore a cross on their uniforms to show that they were Christians. To distinguish them from the other orders of Knights, their cross had four triangular arms. It was later called the Maltese Cross.

1576 Rudolf II becomes Holy Roman emperor (to 1612) on the death of his father, Maximilian II. In the Pacification of Ghent, all the provinces of the Netherlands unite to drive out the Spaniards. Protestantism is forbidden in France. India: Akbar, the Mogul emperor, conquers Bengal.

1577 Europe: An alliance is made between England and the Netherlands against Spain. England: Francis Drake sets out to sail round the world. Low Countries: The Flemish painter, Peter Paul Rubens is born (dies 1640).

A sketch of an Indian setting a parrot trap, first drawn by one of the English captain, Francis Drake's companions during his voyage around the world.

1578 The Duke of Parma subdues the southern provinces of the Netherlands. North Africa: Sebastian of Portugal invades Morocco. His troops are defeated and he is killed at the battle of Alcazar. Sebastian has no children and is succeeded by Cardinal Henry. The Cardinal asks the pope's permission to marry so he can start a new dynasty.

1579 Netherlands: The Northern provinces form the Union of Utrecht to fight against Spain. India: The Portuguese set up trading colonies in Bengal.

1580 Portugal: Cardinal Henry dies. Philip II of Spain, Sebastian's uncle, invades and declares himself king. Francis Drake returns to England after sailing round the world. The Moguls invade Afghanistan.

1581 The United Provinces of the Netherlands, declare themselves independent of Spain and elect William of Orange as their ruler. Russia: Ivan the Terrible kills his eldest son in a fit of rage. Poland invades Russia.

Dutch Independence

The Netherlands were made up of 17 provinces in what is now Belgium, Luxembourg and the Netherlands. From 1482 to 1506 they were ruled by Philip of Burgundy, son of the Holy Roman Emperor. Philip's son, Charles, inherited them and made them a Spanish possession when he became king of Spain in 1516.

The fight for independence started after Charles's son became King Philip II of Spain. He strongly resisted the Protestant threat to Catholicism and tried to take complete power over the Low Countries. In 1567 Philip made the Duke of Alba governor of the Netherlands with orders to use terror to crush any opposition. The Duke of Alba started by executing two leaders of the opposition and this led to the Dutch Revolts led by

▼ *The Netherlands were called the Low Countries, because they were low-lying lands, close to the sea. They became rich through trade in the 16th century.*

WILLIAM OF ORANGE

1533 Born.
1544 Becomes Prince of Orange.
1559 Governs Holland, Zeeland and Utrecht.
1567–1572 Leads the Dutch Revolts.
1573 Joins the Calvinist church.
1580 Philip II declares him an outlaw.
1584 A Catholic fanatic assassinates William.

▲ *Amsterdam's wealth grew after 1576. The city was built largely on land reclaimed from the sea. It consisted of more than 100 islands linked by canals.*

▶ *A caricature (exaggerated drawing) of the Duke of Alba trying to stamp out heresy in the Netherlands by trampling on the bodies of executed Protestants.*

William of Orange. As Alba became more ruthless, so the opposition spread. There were public executions. Towns were pillaged and their populations massacred. In 1576 Spanish troops sacked Antwerp, ending its prosperity. Many merchants and bankers moved to Amsterdam.

Spain brought the southern provinces back under its control, but in 1581 seven northern provinces declared themselves independent. These provinces were where most of the Protestants lived. Under William of Orange, they called themselves the Republic of the United Netherlands, but Spain did not recognize their independence until 1648.

Trade

In the 16th century the most important trading centres in Europe were Antwerp and Amsterdam. Wool from England and grain, fish and timber from the Baltic reached the growing population of Europe through these cities. New markets were opening up for goods produced on a large scale such as woollen cloth, iron goods and firearms.

Spain's exploitation of its South American empire meant a flood of silver into Europe. This encouraged business but it also brought inflation. The first African slaves were taken to the Americas in 1502. The need for cheap labour led to more and more Africans being taken there to work.

▲ *Quentin Massys painted this picture* The Moneychanger and his Wife *in 1500. For a small sum gold was exchanged for silver coins or one currency for another.*

▶ *Europe suffered rapid inflation. Prices rose by up to 400 per cent in ninety years.*

◀ *China attracted many visitors, but not all of them were as welcome as these going to Beijing. European traders were regarded as little better than pirates. The Chinese were prepared to sell silk and porcelain, but they did not want European goods in exchange.*

WHEN IT HAPPENED

1460s The Portuguese set up forts in Africa to trade in gold, silver and ivory.

1498 Vasco da Gama becomes the first European to reach India by sea.

1502 The first African slaves are taken to South America by Spanish settlers. They are used as a source of cheap labour on plantations.

1576 Antwerp is sacked by Spanish troops.

1600 In England the East India Company is set up to trade with India.

▲ As trade increased in Europe, towns and cities grew larger. In London, shops, houses and inns were even built on London Bridge. The weight of them caused many maintenance problems.

◄ Ship navigation was very basic at this time. Some captains relied on the Sun and stars. Others used a compass and charts when possible. They told the time on board with a sandglass in which the sand took half an hour to run through. They could also use a board like this to tell the time by the stars at night.

▼ Russia was cut off from Europe for nearly 250 years. In the late 15th century Russian merchants like these, by order of the tsar, began establishing links in fur trading.

► A Portuguese map, drawn in 1558. Maps showing sea routes were jealously guarded to stop other countries stealing them and taking the trade.

389

North America

When the Europeans first arrived in America in the 16th century, there were hundreds of different tribes of native people living there. Each tribe had its own customs, language and way of life, according to where it lived. For example, on the Great Plains where wild animals were plentiful, the North American Indians lived by hunting and trapping. The animals they caught provided them with meat and also with skins to make into clothing and shelters. Tribes who lived on the coast or by lakes where trees were plentiful, made wooden canoes and went fishing.

In the south-west, people living in villages called *pueblos* grew crops of maize (corn), squash (pumpkin) and beans by building dams to irrigate the dry land. They also set up trading links with the Aztecs and other native peoples.

Native North Americans on the east coast also lived by farming. They grew maize and tobacco in plots around their villages. The people hunted and trapped animals and gathered fruit, nuts and

▲ The Miami tribe made clothing from hides and furs. First the skins were cleaned and stretched, then cut and sewn into garments and moccasins. In many tribes women were responsible for raising crops while men hunted. Women, however, did play an important part in tribal affairs; some became chiefs while others took part in tribal councils, held to settle quarrels.

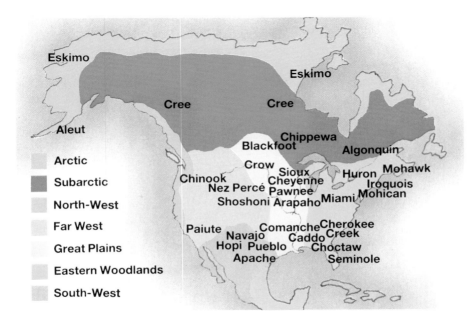

Eskimo

Eskimo

Cree   Cree

Aleut

Chippewa
Blackfoot   Algonquin

Crow   Sioux   Huron   Mohawk
Chinook   Cheyenne   Iroquois
    Nez Percé Pawnee   Mohican
Shoshoni Arapaho Miami

                Cherokee
Paiute   Comanche Creek
    Navajo   Caddo
Hopi Pueblo   Choctaw
    Apache   Seminole

Arctic

Subarctic

North-West

Far West

Great Plains

Eastern Woodlands

South-West

◄ The map shows where the main tribes of Native North Americans lived in 1500, before Europeans arrived and started driving them off their lands. At that time there were between one and six million Native North Americans. They did not believe that they 'owned' the land but thought that it was held in common for the entire tribe. The coloured areas shown indicate regions in which tribes shared a similar way of life.

▲ Hunters on the Great Plains sometimes camouflaged (disguised) themselves in animal skins when they went in search of prey.

▲ The Chippewas lived in wigwams. The frame was made from bent branches and covered with an outer layer of animal skin or birch bark.

berries from the surrounding forests.

Like the Aztecs and the Incas, none of these tribes knew about the horse or wheeled transport before the Europeans arrived. Their knowledge of metal was also very limited and most of their tools were made from either wood or stone. Their main weapon was the bow and arrow. It was used for hunting and also in occasional wars between tribes.

The arrival of the Europeans in the late 16th and early 17th centuries soon had a disastrous effect on all these tribes. Many died from diseases, such as smallpox and measles, which had been unknown in America up to then. Others were killed in disputes and the rest were gradually driven off their lands.

1582 Europe: The Gregorian calendar is introduced into Roman Catholic countries. Peace is declared between Russia, Poland and Sweden. Mogul empire: Akbar abolishes slavery.

1583 North America: The English explorer Humphrey Gilbert takes possession of Newfoundland on behalf of Queen Elizabeth and founds the first English settlement in the Americas.

1584 North America: Sir Walter Raleigh names Virginia after Queen Elizabeth I. Netherlands: William of Orange is murdered. England sends aid to the Netherlands. Switzerland: Bern, Geneva and Zurich form an alliance against the Roman Catholic cantons. Russia: Ivan the Terrible dies and is succeeded by his second son, Fyodor (to 1598).

1585 Papal States: Sixtus V is elected as pope (to 1590). France: the 'War of the Three Henrys' starts. Japan: Hideyoshi comes to power in Japan. Low Countries: The Dutch use the first time bombs at the seige of Antwerp.

1586 England: Mary, Queen of Scots is involved in a plot against Elizabeth I. Persia: Abbas I becomes shah (to 1628). India: Akbar conquers Kashmir.

1587 England: Mary, Queen of Scots is executed. England is at war with Spain. Sir Francis Drake destroys the Spanish fleet at Cadiz. Savoy and the Catholic cantons form an alliance with Spain.

The tribes of the Iroquois wore masks during important tribal ceremonies. They represented mythological creatures.

1588 The Spanish Armada is defeated by the English fleet under Lord Howard of Effingham, Sir Francis Drake and Sir John Hawkins, but the war between Spain and England continues (to 1603). France: Henry of Guise is murdered.

Japan and China

In 1467 civil war broke out among the great feudal lords of Japan. The emperor had lost most of his power and even the shogun had very little influence over the running of the country. For over 100 years private armies of samurai fought against each other in the struggle to control Japan.

During these civil wars, Europeans started visiting Japan. The first to arrive were Portuguese sailors in 1542. Seven years later a Spanish missionary, St Francis Xavier, arrived to try and convert the Japanese to Christianity. Other traders and missionaries followed and were made welcome at first.

As well as introducing a new religion to Japan, the Europeans also brought firearms. Some samurai looked down on these, saying they were the weapons of cowards, but others quickly saw their advantages in battle.

One samurai called Oda Nobunaga equipped his men with muskets (guns) and captured Kyoto in 1568. His own efforts to reunite Japan ended when he was killed, but his work was continued

▲ When he was shogun, Hideyoshi managed to break the power of the feudal lords and the Buddhist monks, but his plans for an empire failed.

by Hideyoshi. He became shogun in 1585 and planned to built a great Japanese empire which would include China. Hideyoshi invaded Korea twice, in 1592 and 1597, but failed to conquer it. The second campaign was abandoned when Hideyoshi died. Hideyoshi had appointed Tokugawa Ieyasu his son's guardian and on his death a power struggle broke out. Civil war followed until Ieyasu defeated his rivals at the battle of Sekigahara in 1600, becoming shogun in 1603.

▼ At the battle of Nagashino in 1575, Nobunaga armed his 3000 men with muskets. They were able to defeat a much larger force of mounted samurai, armed with a mixture of swords, bows and arrows.

By 1500 the Ming dynasty in China was weakening. The emperor forbade Chinese ships to sail beyond coastal waters, but allowed foreign ships to visit China. From 1517 Portuguese and other Europeans traders visited the coast. In 1557 the Portuguese were allowed to settle in Macao and some Jesuit priests were allowed into Beijing. The expense of defeating Hideyoshi's invasion of Korea in 1592 helped to destabilize China. A time of famine also led to unrest and in the 17th century the Manchus invaded from the north.

◀ *Missionaries from Europe had converted 150,000 Japanese to Christianity by the year 1580. This lessened the power of the Buddhists, whom the Japanese ruler Hideyoshi distrusted. But later he regarded Christianity as a dangerous threat to Japanese beliefs. In 1587 Christianity was banned and Christians were persecuted and put to death.*

TEA CEREMONY

The Japanese tea ceremony is called *cha-no-yu*. It was originally brought to Japan by Buddhist monks from China, but the ceremony spread beyond the monasteries in the 15th century. Japanese society was very formal, so strict rules developed over the way the tea was prepared, served and drunk. The ceremony had to take place in a simple but elegant room. A tea master was in charge.

1589 France: Henry III of France is murdered and the Protestant leader Henry of Navarre succeeds as Henry IV (to 1610).

1590 Near East: Peace is declared between the Ottoman and Safavid empires. England: Around this time Shakespeare begins writing plays. Netherlands: The first microscope is made by Hans and Zacharias Janssen. India: Akbar, the Mogul emperor, conquers Sindh.

A Chinese mine-layer barge.

1591 West Africa: The Songhay empire is destroyed by Spanish and Portuguese mercenaries in the service of Morocco.

1592 Papal States: Clement VIII becomes pope (to 1605). Japan: Hideyoshi invades Korea with plans to conquer China, but is forced to withdraw the following year.

1593 War starts between Austria and the Ottoman empire.

1595 The Treaty of Teusina between Sweden and Russia, gives Sweden Estonia.

1597 Ireland: Under Hugh O'Neill, Earl of Tyrone, the Irish rebel again.

1598 The Edict of Nantes ends civil wars in France by giving Huguenots equal political rights with Roman Catholics. Spain: Philip II dies and his son becomes Philip III (to 1621). Russia: On the death of Fyodor, Boris Godunov becomes tsar (to 1605). Persia: Abbas I drives out the Uzbek Turks.

1599 Ireland: Irish rebels defeat the Earl of Essex and his English army.

1600 England: The East India Company is founded. Ireland: The king of Spain sends an army to support the Earl of Tyrone's rebellion.

War and Weapons

In Europe the increasing use of gunpowder meant that castles were no longer an adequate defence against the enemy. This led to more open battles, instead of the long sieges there had been in the Middle Ages. Both cannons and handguns were used adding artillery to the two divisions of infantry and cavalry. Although the flintlock was developed, firearms were not very reliable and often injured the person firing them rather than the enemy.

Most soldiers lived in poor conditions. They were often underfed and underpaid. They were also poorly disciplined and more likely to die from disease than enemy fire.

▲ *The warrior ruler of Japan, Hideyoshi, built Himeji castle in 1577. It was his stronghold in the civil wars which tore Japan apart for almost 100 years.*

◄ *Aztec warriors decorated their ceremonial shields with bright feathers. This one was a gift sent to Spain in the early 1500s.*

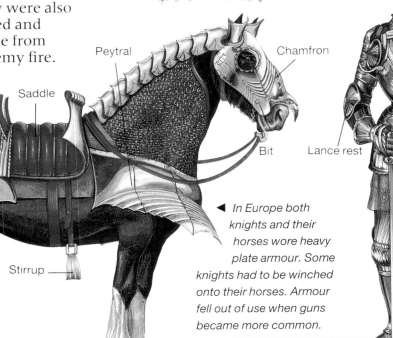

Crupper

Saddle

Peytral

Chamfron

Bit

Stirrup

Visor

Breast plat

Lance rest

Leg harne

◄ *In Europe both knights and their horses wore heavy plate armour. Some knights had to be winched onto their horses. Armour fell out of use when guns became more common.*

1526 The battle of Panipat in India. Babur founds the Mogul empire.

1525 At the battle of Flodden Field Scotland is heavily defeated by England. The Scottish king James IV is killed in the battle.

1571 The sea-battle of Lepanto takes place in the Mediterranean. Although the fleet of the Holy League is outnumbered they defeat the Ottoman navy in three hours.

1578 The king of Portugal is killed in battle against the Moroccans.

▼ *In 1520 Henry VIII of England and Francis I of France met in Flanders at the 'Field of the Cloth of Gold' to make an alliance between their countries. Instead the event turned into a contest between the two kings with each trying to outdo the other in the splendour of his arrival.*

▶ *Most European armies were made up of professional soldiers who assembled groups of mercenaries for hire to the highest bidder. Many mercenaries found work in South-East Asia, along the trade routes. This Mogul miniature shows Portuguese mercenaries fighting the Indians.*

The Calendar Change

The calendar which is used in almost every part of the world today is known as the Gregorian calendar. This is because it was worked out by the astronomers of Pope Gregory XIII in the 16th century. Before then Europeans used the Julian calendar, established by Julius Caesar in 46 BC.

In this calendar a period of three years, each of 365 days, was followed by a leap year with 366 days. This meant that the average length of a year was 365.25 days. However, the amount of time which the Earth actually takes to orbit the Sun is 365.2422 days. This made a year in the Julian calendar 11 minutes and 14 seconds longer than the actual year, and so an extra day appeared about every 128 years.

By the 1580s the Julian calendar was 10 days ahead of the seasons. To correct this, Pope Gregory made 5 October 1582 into 15 October. To prevent the error happening again, he decided that every year which could be divided by four would be a leap year with 366 days. Every century year divisible by 400 (such as 1600) would also be a leap year.

Roman Catholic countries adopted the new calendar at once, but many Protestant kingdoms did not change until 1700. Britain altered its calendar in 1752, by which time there was a difference of 11 days. Russia kept the Julian calendar until 1918.

The use of different calendars in the 16th century can be very confusing. For example, the date when the Spanish Armada was seen off the coast of England can differ by ten days, depending on whether a Spaniard or an English person recorded it. Also, in England, the New Year started on March 25, and not January 1, until the Gregorian calendar came into use.

▲ *All through the centuries, scholars tried to find ways of measuring the passage of time. On this 13th century French manuscript they are comparing the lunar (Moon) year with the solar (Sun) year.*

ROMAN CALENDAR

As well as calculating the Julian calendar, the Romans divided the year into 12 months. To this day the names for them are based on the Roman ones. January was named after Janus, the two-headed god of beginnings who could look both ways at once. February was named after *februa*, a Roman feast which took place at that time. March was named after Mars, the god of war, and April comes from the Latin *aperire* (to open) as it is the month when the earth opens up to produce new plants. May is named after the goddess Maia and June after the goddess Juno. July takes its name from Julius Caesar and August from Augustus Caesar. September, October, November and December were originally the seventh, eighth, ninth and tenth months.